THE DIARY OF OLGA ROMANOV

THE DIARY OF

Olga Romanov

ROYAL WITNESS

TO THE

RUSSIAN REVOLUTION

With Excerpts from Family Letters and Memoirs of the Period

HELEN AZAR

WESTHOLME
Yardley

Westholme Publishing, LLC
904 Edgewood Road
Yardley, Pennsylvania 19067
Visit our Web site at www.westholmepublishing.com

First Printing November 2013
10 9 8 7 6 5 4 3 2 1
ISBN: 978-1-59416-177-3
Also available as an eBook.

Printed in the United States of America.

CONTENTS

(A gallery of images appears after page 66)

PROLOGUE

S verdlovsk Region, the Urals, Russia. May 1979. A small investigation team weaved its way through a forest toward a lonely meadow in search of a very special burial site. Led by Alexander Avdonin, a retired geologist, and accompanied by Geli Ryabov, a filmmaker for the Ministry of Interior Affairs, and a fellow geologist, Michael Kochurov, the team had been searching for answers to sixty-year-old historical questions.

In a clearing about four and a half miles from the Four Brothers mine shaft, in an area curiously called the Piglet Meadow, they came upon a shallow grave. They realized that this must be what they had been looking for. Having dug down just a few feet they came upon what appeared to be human bones, and indeed these turned out to be the remains of nine skeletons.

Slowly, one by one, Avdonin and his fellow researchers unearthed three skulls and washed them with water from a nearby spring. The skulls looked gray and black and in some areas appeared to be damaged with acid. The center facial bones of the skulls were missing and had large round holes, as if smashed in by some hard object. Avdonin and his team instinctively knew that this was the groundbreaking historical discovery they were after. It was also a finding they realized could endanger them and their families. They decided to rebury the skulls in the original gravesite and to keep quiet about their find until circumstances in the country changed.

The right time came a little more than a decade later. By the early 1990s the Soviet Union had fallen and the new ideology of openness allowed the Russian people to ask questions about their history without fear of retribution. One of the most nagging unanswered questions was what happened to Russia's last ruler—Tsar Nicholas II—and his family, who were arrested in 1918 and were thought to be murdered near Sverdlovsk, then known as Ekaterinburg. For many years there were no bodies to prove that these deaths actually occurred. For more than a half a century of Soviet rule, the lack of detailed information surrounding the fate of the murdered imperial family gave rise to numerous rumors of conspiracies and various survivors, not just in Russia but also in the West. Individuals periodically surfaced claiming to be one imperial daughter or another, the former heir, or even the tsar himself. There were movies, cartoons, and books based on the alleged survival of the most famous of all imperial daughters—the Grand Duchess Anastasia, which helped reignite twenty-first century interest in the last Russian imperial family. Under the Soviet regime the subject was all but forbidden, but times had certainly changed and people's natural curiosity about the last imperial family seemed to be almost encouraged.

Russian president Boris Yeltsin finally authorized an official scientific opening of the Piglet Meadow burial site in 1991, while Governor Edward Rossel, the chairman of the Sverdlovsk Region Executive Committee, formally announced to the press the discovery of the bones which "in great probability" belonged to Nicholas Romanov—the former Tsar of Russia—and his wife, three of his five children, and several of their servants.

In July 1992, a team of forensic specialists under the direction of Dr. William Maples from the University of Florida arrived in the former Sverdlovsk, which had now reverted to its previous name, Ekaterinburg. The scientists quickly determined that these were indeed the remains of the last Russian imperial family. Concurrently, Russian forensics scientists, using digital computer images to compare old photographs of the imperial family to the skulls, announced that they had been successful in superimposing the sets of photos, thus demonstrating that the remains belonged to the Romanov family.

A few years later, in the United Kingdom, Dr. Peter Gill of Biology Research Science Laboratory performed DNA tests comparing the Ekaterinburg remains to Prince Philip, Duke of Edinburgh, who is one of the closest maternal living relatives of Tsarina Alexandra and her children. Similar DNA profile studies were also carried out in the United States by Dr. Mary-Claire King of the University of California at Berkeley, as well as by the U.S. Armed Forces Institute of Pathology in Rockville, Maryland.

All the DNA analyses were completed in the autumn of 1995 and confirmed beyond any scientific doubt that the skeletal remains belonged to the Romanovs. Among the remains were ones which belonged to the eldest daughter of Nicholas II, the Grand Duchess Olga Nikolaevna Romanov—aged twenty-two at the time of her death.

The discovery and scientific identification of the Ekaterinburg remains should have put to rest all the conspiracy theories and fairy tales about the final fate of the tsar and his family. But astonishingly the controversy continued, not least of all because the Russian Orthodox Church, along with one of the branches of the surviving extended Romanov family, refused to accept the definitive scientific results which proved that the remains found near Ekaterinburg indeed belonged to the murdered imperial family. Reason prevailed and in July 1998, the remains of Grand Duchess Olga, her parents, and two of her sisters were interred in the imperial family crypt at the St. Peter and St. Paul Cathedral on the eightieth anniversary of their execution. The Romanov family was at last in their final resting place among their royal ancestors. It was not until nearly ten years later when the remains of Aleksei and the fourth sister were finally found not far from where the others were first discovered. The eighty-year-old mystery of what happened to the bodies of the last Russian imperial family was solved.

RUSSIA AND THE ROMANOVS
BEFORE WORLD WAR I

In the dawn of 1905, less than a year after the birth of the long-awaited heir to the Russian throne, the Romanov dynasty teetered on the brink of disaster. On the morning of January 9, imperial troops opened fire on citizens who had gathered in protest in Palace Square in St. Petersburg. The protesters had refused to disperse until they could present a petition for reforms to their tsar, Nicholas II. In what became known in Russian history as "Bloody Sunday," hundreds of unarmed St. Petersburg workers were shot and killed and thousands more wounded.

That very day, the myth of "the good tsar," who cared and wished to protect his people, bled to death in the snow in front of the Winter Palace along with the victims of the mass shooting. A new term, "Bloody Nicholas," was born, branding the tsar as the ruthless autocrat who ordered the deaths of hundreds of innocent citizens who had gathered together to ask for his help to bring about better working conditions.

Bloody Sunday, coupled with the disastrous war with Japan the previous year, caused the popularity of Tsar Nicholas II to plummet. It did not matter that Nicholas and his family were not even present in St. Petersburg that day, or that the tsar did not even learn of the tragedy until well after it was over. He was now seen by many of his subjects as a heartless tyrant with the blood of innocent Russian people on his hands. The events led to massive general strikes and political unrest across Russia, and ultimately Nicholas II had to make some unprecedented constitutional concessions in order to save his position, as well as the Romanov dynasty. The year 1905 is in fact considered by many historians to be the first Russian revolution.

Nicholas began his reign in the autumn of 1894, the second Russian emperor by that name and a direct descendant of Empress Catherine the Great. His accession occurred much sooner than anyone had expected. Nicholas's father, Tsar Alexander III, died unexpectedly at the relatively young age of forty-nine.

Events unfolded rapidly after the passing of Alexander. The new tsar, aged twenty-six, quickly married his fiancé of several months, Princess Alix of Hesse—the granddaughter of Queen Victoria of England. The couple knew each other from adolescence. They were even distantly related and had numerous relatives in common, being the niece and nephew of the Prince and Princess of Wales, from different sides of the family.

Upon her marriage, Princess Alix converted from Lutheranism to Russian Orthodoxy, as stipulated by canon law, and was renamed Alexandra Fedorovna. The new Russian empress had grown up in a very different world: the quiet duchy of Hesse on the Rhine, the youngest surviving daughter of its grand duke. When Alix was just six years old, her mother, Princess Alice, one of Queen Victoria's daughters, died of diphtheria at the age of thirty-six. At the same time, Alix lost her younger sister and playmate from the same disease. The untimely deaths of the people closest to her greatly affected the girl. Never again was she the sunny and carefree child she had been prior to the tragedy.

Alix was twelve years old when she first met the young Tsesarevich Nicholas, the heir to the Russian throne, when in 1884 she and her family traveled to Russia to attend the wedding of her older sister, Elisabeth. Grand Duchess Elisabeth Fedorovna, as she was now known, married one of Nicholas's uncles, the Grand Duke Sergei Alexandrovich.

In the nineteenth century, many members of the European royal families were closely related to each other. Queen Victoria was referred to as "the grandmother of Europe" because her progeny were dispersed throughout the continent through the marriages of her numerous children. Along with her royal pedigree and improved diplomatic relations among the royal houses of Greece, Spain, Germany, and Russia, Victoria's descendants received something much less desirable: a tiny defect in a gene that regulates normal blood clotting and causes an incurable medical condition called hemophilia. At that time patients suffering from this disease could literally bleed to death. Even the most benign bruise or bump might prove fatal. Victoria's own son Leopold was a hemophiliac who died prematurely after a minor fall.

The hemophilia gene was also passed on to Victoria's male grandchildren and great-grandchildren through their mothers in Spain and Germany. Alix's own brother died of complications from hemophilia at the age of three when he suffered relatively minor injuries after accidentally falling out of a window.

But arguably the most tragic and significant effect of the hemophilia gene occurred in the imperial house of Russia. Because the Russian legal code contained a statute known as Salic law, only males could inherit the throne. If Nicholas did not have a son, the crown would pass to his younger brother

Michael. However, after ten years of marriage and the births of four healthy grand duchesses, Nicholas and Alexandra had the long-awaited son and heir, only to discover that he was stricken by an incurable ailment. Not many subjects realized that their new tsesarevich's life often hung by a thread due to his deadly genetic inheritance. Aleksei's hemophilia remained a closely guarded secret.

The family doted on the little boy; he was overprotected and spoiled. In 1912, when Aleksei was eight years old, he came close to death after a minor accident while the family was on a holiday in Poland. Aleksei's life was apparently saved by the intervention of a Siberian peasant named Grigori Rasputin. It was not the first time that Rasputin's seemingly miraculous powers had been evoked. On this occasion, Rasputin had not even been present in Poland but had communicated via telegraph from his own home in Siberia.

An obituary to announce the passing of the heir to the throne had already been prepared, and the imperial doctors had all but given up on the seemingly dying boy. But amazingly, Aleksei slowly recovered after Rasputin's telephone call. Hence the man whom Aleksei's parents referred to as "Our Friend" and "Father Grigori" solidified his role as the savior of their beloved son, as well as their own spiritual advisor whom they viewed as their liaison with God.

During the summer of 1913, the Romanov dynasty commemorated its tercentennial. The dark "times of trouble" of 1905 seemed like a long-forgotten and unpleasant dream. To celebrate, the tsar and his family made a pilgrimage to ancient historical landmarks around the Moscow region, and the people cheered. Nicholas and Alexandra were once again convinced that their people loved them and that their policies were on the right track.

It would have been difficult for anyone to imagine at this time that only four years after these days of glory, a revolution would depose the Romanov dynasty from its imperial throne. The family that was hailed enthusiastically during the celebrations of 1913 would no longer rule Russia in 1917. Instead, they would be under arrest, and a little more than a year after that they would be dead—murdered by their own people.

Numerous factors influenced the events that led to the sudden end of a three-hundred-year-old Russian imperial dynasty. Terrible losses during World War I and continuous rumors and a widespread belief that Rasputin was ruling Russia through his influence on the imperial couple were among the reasons that events spiraled out of control. The bloody climax came on the night of July 17, 1918, when a Bolshevik execution squad shot, bludgeoned, and bayoneted the tsar and his family to death.

It is difficult to say whether history would have been different if the baby boy who was destined to inherit the Russian crown had been born as healthy as his sisters. Would the historical outcome for Russia and the world have been any different? Clearly the nature of Aleksei's medical condition contributed in many ways to the downfall of the Romanov dynasty. Their son's hemophilia was one of the main reasons Nicholas and Alexandra isolated themselves in Tsarskoe Selo, trying their best to keep the heir's condition secret not only from their subjects but even from their extended family members. Aleksei's hemophilia was the principal cause of Alexandra's terrible anxieties and various physical ailments, real or imagined. These led her to avoid society, thus alienating the imperial family from their subjects. This uncharacteristic behavior was misinterpreted by Russia's aristocratic upper class and antagonized those who might have supported Nicholas and Alexandra during difficult times. The isolation of the tsar's family fostered a climate of misunderstanding, frustration, and ultimately resentment.

Perhaps if more people in Russia had known about Aleksei's hemophilia, they would have not harbored some of the suspicions and sinister innuendos arising from the close relationship of Alexandra, in particular, with the hated Siberian peasant. The degree of Grigori Rasputin's influence, while certainly great, was in fact exaggerated. But often perception becomes reality.

There is no denying that Aleksei's hemophilia was the principal reason why Rasputin came into the lives of the Russian imperial family in the first place. He inadvertently but significantly contributed to discrediting Nicholas as a ruler among his subjects during a major war, which led to the tsar's abdication and to his and his family's eventual deaths.

The story of the last reigning Romanovs continues to fascinate scholars as well as Russian history buffs. In it there is something for everyone: a great royal romance between a handsome young tsar—the ruler of one eighth of the entire world—and a beautiful German princess who gave up her strong Lutheran faith and life as she knew it for love. There were their beautiful children: four lovely daughters, and a baby boy born with a disease from which he could die at any moment. There was the controversial "holy" man who seemed to have wormed his way into the imperial palace, and who was seen to have a corrupt and immoral influence on the tsar, the empress, and their children. There was even an unlikely simpleton, or in some people's opinion a cunning "best friend" to the empress. This was Anna Vyrubova, who allegedly manipulated the empress and even the emperor behind the scenes, in league with Rasputin.

There were political assassinations of the powerful, shootings of the innocent, partisan intrigues, worker strikes, mass uprisings, and a world war; a murder, a revolution, and a bloody civil war. And finally there was regicide: a secret execution in the middle of the night of the tsar, the empress, all of their children, their servants, even their pets, in the cellar of the "House of Special Purpose" in the heart of Russia's Urals.

The last reigning Romanov family unwittingly created a thorough historical legacy. Due to their love of photography, their habit of letter writing, and the tradition of keeping daily diaries, they provided detailed evidence of their lives. Tsar Nicholas, his wife, and all of his children kept diaries, starting at the age of about nine to eleven. The diaries were not in any way intended for pouring out their souls, but rather to keep track of daily events, in an almost subjective manner. Occasionally, emotions and opinions inevitably made their way into the diaries. Many of the diaries were destroyed by their owners when the revolution broke out, but some did survive.

The diaries of the eldest daughter of the tsar, the Grand Duchess Olga Nikolaevna, will be the focus of this book. The original diaries are currently held at GARF (State Archives of Russian Federation) in Fond # 673, op. 1, 271 ed. All the documents contained in this Fond are dated 1895–1917. Fond 673 also contains additional documents which reflect the grand duchess's other activities, connected to her work at the infirmary, her patronage of various committees, military regiments of which she was chief, as well as her correspondence with relatives and friends. The diaries, however, are arguably the most valuable of these documents.

Olga Nikolaevna kept her diaries from the age of nine, writing in Russian. The first entry was made on January 1, 1905 ("I was in church with Papa and Mama"), the last on March 15, 1917, which was almost exactly a year and four months before her death. The rest of the pages from the 1917 book were torn out. It is unclear whether there may have been more writing on the torn-out pages, but judging by the last page this was probably not the case.

There are twelve of Olga's diary books in total. From 1905 until 1912 they are custom-made memorial gift books (9 by 13 inches or 22.86 x 33.02 centimeters), a different color for each year, in silk bindings, with the dates on the cover. From 1913 until 1916 they are contained in large notebooks with dark leather bindings, which fit the entire year plus a few months of the next. The entire 1910 diary is missing—probably burned by Olga after the revolution.

All the diaries consist of short entries about regular events, activities, and meetings kept daily during the year. Only during the early years do we come upon missed entries. As Olga got older, the diary entries were kept more carefully and consistently.

From 1911 on, the grand duchess began using her own special codes. When Crimean researcher Maria Zemlyanichenko read Olga's diaries she was the first to take notice of the abbreviation "S.," which referred to the name of the grand duchess's love interest. Upon closer inspection this seemed to be a letter referring to a person's nickname rather than their given name. Knowing that the imperial family liked to use affectionate nicknames for each other, like "Sunny" or "Sunshine," we can speculate that this is what this letter may have stood for. Her beloved was her "Sunshine," who brought light into her somewhat monotonous world. Different codes referred to other love interests.

In the diaries we can follow how these crushes became real psychological attachments: she longs to see "him" all the time, be near "him," misses "him." And she is always full of happiness when she does see her "dear one," "charming one," "golden one." When Olga's diaries are compared to other journals, it is possible to figure out some of the names of the mysterious love interests and other secret codes. Some of the decoded lines are included in this book.

Starting in August 1914, the events of World War I and the work with the wounded at the infirmary where Olga worked as a nurse filled her entire life. This is clearly reflected in her writings. Her empathy toward the wounded soldiers who fought for their country, her loyalty to Russia, love for her parents and siblings, and her strong religious faith are always evident in her diary entries.

Olga and her three younger sisters collectively referred to themselves as "OTMA," an acronym for the first four letters of their respective names: Olga, Tatiana, Maria, and Anastasia. Their brother Aleksei was usually viewed as a separate entity, not just because he was the only boy, but also due to his grand status as the heir to the Russian throne.

One of the most famous Russian rulers was Empress Catherine the Great. Why could not the eldest daughter of the tsar inherit the throne? The answer goes back several generations. After the death of his mother, Catherine's son, Tsar Paul I, quickly instated the Salic law because of his hatred toward the late empress. Paul wanted to prevent any other woman from ruling Russia again.

If it were not for the Salic law, the eldest imperial daughter would have been recognized as the heir presumptive and become empress in the absence of a legitimate male heir. In the case of Nicholas and Alexandra, there would not have been an imperative to keep trying for a son, and later to ensure the son's survival at any cost, at least not for political reasons. In 1917 the tsar abdicated; the fact that a daughter could not inherit the throne, coupled with Aleksei's delicate health, meant that this spelled the end of the Romanov dynasty.

Again, there is no way to tell how differently history would have turned out if the Salic law had not prevented Olga, or one of her sisters, from being crowned as empress. This young woman was a witness to historical events, and if certain decisions and actions of her forebears had been different, Olga might have played a much more significant role in the history of not only Russia but most likely the entire world.

As things actually stood in 1917–18, Grand Duchess Olga was relatively irrelevant in political terms. She was murdered along with her parents and siblings not because of what she did or could have done, but because of who she was.

The surviving diaries of all of Nicholas II's daughters were kept under strict supervision in Russian archives until very recently. Most of them have not been translated into English or published at all. This book contains translations of representative excerpts from Grand Duchess Olga's diary covering the time period 1914–1917, from World War I to the Russian Revolution. It also includes some previously unpublished letters to her father during the same time period. Where Olga's diary abruptly leaves off, I have allowed Nicholas II to continue the story with his own diaries, supplemented by memoirs written by close family friends and associates and other documents pertaining to the period. The memoirs of close family friends and associates such as Anna Vyrubova, and such major players as the head of the Provisional Government Alexander Kerensky are included in the narrative, to offer a wider perspective of the events. This is the first time most of these documents have been translated into English and published.

THE CHILDHOOD OF
OLGA ROMANOV

We know little about this great-granddaughter of Queen Victoria. We have seen pictures of her sitting with her sisters, standing alone in Court dress, or on horseback in the uniform of her regiment. We have heard details of her life, of her devotion to her sisters, her parents, her little brother, but few know that her mentality, her intelligence, her gifts, would have made her a remarkable personality, had she lived.—Meriel Buchanan

Who was the Grand Duchess Olga Nikolaevna Romanova? The daughter of the British ambassador, Meriel Buchanan, talks about the Grand Duchess Olga as a figure of considerable mystery during her short life. Olga's own diaries give remarkable insight into the life and times of the eldest daughter of Russia's last tsar.

A very large baby girl came into the world on November 15 (old style[1]: November 3) 1895, in St. Petersburg, Russia. On that day her father, Tsar Nicholas II, wrote in his diary:

1. The Gregorian calendar (new style) replaced the Julian calendar (old style) in Catholic countries beginning in 1582. This change was also implemented in Protestant and Orthodox countries after a significant delay. In Russia the change took place after the revolution in 1918.

"A day I will remember forever . . . at exactly 9 o'clock a baby's cry was heard and we all breathed a sigh of relief! With prayer we named the daughter sent to us by God 'Olga'!"

Olga's aunt the Grand Duchess Ksenia wrote a more cynical diary entry for November 3: "The birth of a daughter to Nicky and Alix! A great joy, although it's a great pity it's not a son! . . . The baby is huge—weighing 10 pounds—and had to be pulled out with forceps!"

Grand Duchess Olga Nikolaevna Romanova was the first of Tsar Nicholas II's and Tsarina Alexandra Fedorovna's five children. Born at the Anichkov Palace, Nicholas's childhood home where the newlywed imperial couple initially settled, Olga was born "in the purple"—during the imperial reign of her parents. Her Russian title "Velikaya Knyazhna" is most precisely translated as "the Grand Princess," which means that Olga, as an "Imperial Highness," was higher in rank than other princesses in Europe who were merely "Royal Highnesses." "Grand Duchess" is the more common English translation.

Olga's mother, Alexandra, startled her own grandmother, Queen Victoria of England, by insisting on breastfeeding her firstborn, which was quite unusual for aristocratic, let alone royal, women in the nineteenth century. Olga was the only one of her siblings to meet in person her formidable English great-grandmother, who was also one of her godmothers. The tiny grand duchess was probably too young to remember her visit to the British court, as it occurred during the family's trip abroad when she was just an infant. Empress Alexandra, known to her family as Alix, was one of Queen Victoria's favorite granddaughters. Victoria was delighted to meet her new great-granddaughter and spend time with her, posing for numerous photos.

As Olga grew into a toddler in 1897, she became the big sister to another imperial daughter, Tatiana. Later in her diaries Olga would refer to herself and her sister Tatiana as "We 2." The two girls were very close in age and did most activities together, and were often dressed in matching outfits.

In 1898, the growing family finally moved away from the Anichkov Palace in St. Petersburg, where they resided with Olga's grandmother, the dowager empress. They made the relatively intimate Alexander Palace in Tsarskoe Selo (literally "Imperial Village," a St. Petersburg suburb) their permanent home. In another year, Olga was joined by yet another baby sister, Maria.

In 1901, just before Olga and her family went on holiday to Peterhof, a seaside town on the Gulf of Finland founded by Peter the Great, she came down with typhoid fever. This was the same disease that killed Olga's great-grandfather Prince Albert, Queen Victoria's consort. The six-year-old grand duchess, seriously ill for five long, weary weeks, was nursed by her mother and her governess, Margaret Eagar. For a while it seemed that Olga might not recover, but she did. Olga was still in bed when her youngest sister, Anastasia, was born. Olga was disappointed at not being able to attend the new baby's baptism, which would have been her first "official" ceremony.

As the young imperial family kept expanding, Olga's parents did their best to provide "normal" lives for their daughters. Just like any Russian family they celebrated Orthodox holidays such as Christmas by exchanging gifts and decorating a fir tree. Eagar, who had been the girls' governess since 1898, remembered in her memoirs one particular Christmas when the young grand duchesses were delighted to see their mother gorgeously attired for a ceremony. They circled around her in speechless admiration when suddenly Olga clapped her hands, and exclaimed fervently, "Oh! Mama, you are just like a lovely Christmas tree!"

The children made Christmas and birthday presents for their parents with their own hands, generally needlework. One Christmas, despite Eagar's attempts to convince her otherwise, Olga insisted on making a kettle-holder for her father. It had a picture of a little kettle singing on a fire, which she embroidered a blue frame around, and the little girl was very happy with her accomplishment. When Christmas came, she presented it to her father, saying, "Nanny was afraid that it wasn't going to be much use to you because it's a kettle-holder, but you can put it on your table and use it as a place mat, or hang it on the wall for a picture. Just see the pretty little frame around it."

From the many intimate anecdotes of her governess, we get a glimpse of Olga's mentality as a little girl. Especially revealing is Olga's attitude about her status as the oldest imperial sibling. The little grand duchess was always profoundly interested in biblical stories, like the one of Joseph and his brothers. After Eagar pronounced how terrible it was for the brothers to be so jealous and so cruel to their youngest sibling, Olga responded, "Joseph was not the eldest, and the beautiful coat should have been given to the eldest son; the other brothers knew that, and perhaps that was why they put him in the pit." All explanations were useless—Olga's sympathies lay with Joseph's eldest brother, Reuben.

A similar incident occurred when a cinematograph was played for the children and some friends. The film showed two little girls playing in a garden, when the older one attempted to snatch a toy from the younger one, who refused to give it up. Foiled in her attempts, the elder girl seized a spoon and pounded the little one with it, which made the latter quickly relinquish the toy and begin to cry. Tatiana was upset and weeping to see the poor little girl so ill-treated, but Olga said, "I am sure that the toy belonged at first to the big sister, and she was kind and lent it to her sister; then she wanted it back, and the little sister would not give it up, so she had to beat her."

When *Alice in Wonderland* was first read to Olga, she was horrified at the manners of the queens. "No queens," Olga said, "would ever be so rude." From books and stories Olga was also able to learn about some things about the outside world that she had never experienced firsthand. When the *Alice in Wonderland* chapter about Alice's journey by railway was read to her, she was very amused that Alice did not have the train compartment all to herself. It was explained to her that each person had to buy a ticket and occupy just one seat in the train, with some tickets costing more than others and the highest-priced tickets granting a better place in the train. Still bemused, Olga asked, "When you travel, can anyone with the same kind of ticket you have get into the same carriage as you do?" No matter how normal her parents tried to make Olga's life, many mundane things that most people took for granted were completely foreign concepts to her.

In 1904, the long-awaited male heir to the Russian throne was born, bringing elation to the imperial family and the entire country. Hence, Olga finally got the chance to participate in her first grand ceremony at the baptism of her baby brother, Aleksei. But the little boy who was destined to become the next tsar of Russia was born with hemophilia, a rare and untreatable blood disorder. The baby boy's condition brought the tight-knit imperial family even closer together, but was also understandably a source of severe anxieties for Olga's parents. Desperation over Aleksei's hemophilia also contributed to the tsar and tsarina's dependence on the reputation of the charismatic Siberian peasant Grigori Rasputin as a faith healer—a factor of major historical significance. As for Olga, she loved her little brother unconditionally, as did Aleksei's other sisters, and felt intensely protective of him.

Even as a child Olga tended to be the most reflective and analytical of her siblings. When she was eight years old, the war between Russia and Japan broke out in 1904. All the girls, even three-year-old Anastasia, worked hard at frame knitting, making scarves for the soldiers, and the two eldest girls also crocheted caps. One day Olga, diligently at work on her crocheting, suddenly said to Margaret Eagar, "I hope the Russian soldiers will kill all the Japanese; not leave even one alive." When the governess explained that there were many innocent children and women in Japan, people who could not fight, Olga reflected for a moment. She then asked her if they also had an emperor in Japan, and hearing that they did, she continued to ask various other questions about Japan. After a pause, Olga finally said slowly, "I did not know that the [Japanese] were people like ourselves." After that conversation, Olga never again said anything about being pleased to hear of the deaths of the Japanese.

When she started to read herself, one of Olga's favorite subjects was stories about medieval European history. According to Eagar, Olga once read a story about the execution of the Welsh Prince Llewellyn. The English beheaded him, sending his head to London, which made a great impression on the little girl. She was terribly shocked, and exclaimed, "It was a good thing he was dead before they cut off his head; it would have hurt him most awfully if he was alive." The governess explained that they were not always so kind and usually cut the heads off living people, to which Olga replied, "I really think people are much better now than they used to be. I'm very glad I live now when people are so kind."

According to her governess, Olga was taught by masters of music as well as Russian and mathematics. Once her arithmetic master, who was a professor of algebra from one of the universities, assigned Olga to write something; she asked his permission to go see the Russian master, who was teaching Tatiana in the next room. When asked why she needed to see him, Olga told him that she wanted to ask him how to spell "arithmetic." The math teacher then spelled this difficult word for her, to which she declared with great admiration, "How clever you are! And how hard you must have studied to be able not only to count so well but to spell such very long words!"

Pierre Gilliard, the grand duchesses' French tutor, described in his memoirs his first meeting with Olga: "The eldest of the Grand Duchesses, Olga, a girl of about ten, [was] very blonde, with eyes full of mischief, and a slightly retroussé little nose; [she] was studying me with an expression that seemed like an attempt to find my weakest point—however, from this child emanated such feeling of purity and sincerity that she immediately gained my sympathy."

Olga was always described as the most intelligent and studious of the imperial siblings, but at the same time the most prone to self-analysis, even melancholy. Around the age of ten in 1905, Olga started recording her thoughts and daily activities in a personal diary in accordance with the imperial family tradition. She kept this diary until March 1917, around the time of her father's abdication from the Russian throne.

Due to her mother's frequent illnesses and dislike of public events, it often fell to Olga, as she grew older, to perform the duties that the tsar's consort would usually do. Of the imperial children, Olga was closest to her father, but she loved both her parents profoundly, as is evident from her diaries. Although she reportedly had occasional differences of opinion with her mother, Olga was fiercely defensive and greatly sympathetic toward her, especially when it came to Alexandra's health.

Much like her father, Olga enjoyed taking long walks in the parks of Tsarskoe Selo. She often said that she would someday live in a small village because she liked nature so much more than the city. Olga also loved to sail on the imperial yacht *Standart*, and enjoyed the annual summer trips to the Black Sea in the Crimea, as well as other family holidays to Finland and Poland.

As Olga grew older, in addition to her love of nature and the outdoors, she became an even more voracious reader of books: the classics, the history of Russia and works detailing the lives of the peasants, ancient traditions, customs, laws, and geography of her nation. She had an extraordinary memory. According to Meriel Buchanan, she never forgot anything that she learned or had been told. Olga also loved music and was an excellent pianist.

Along with her siblings, Olga had keen interest in the lives and problems of others. It was she who once noticed a disabled girl in one of the keepers' cottages in the park at Tsarskoe Selo and insisted on becoming the child's "patron." She made arrangements for the child to be transported to a hospital, and planned on paying for her care out of her own allowance. Of course, Olga had very little knowledge or idea of the value of money. Neither Olga nor any of her siblings ever bought their own clothes or anything else for themselves. The small allowances they received always went toward little presents to their parents or members of their household.

In her memoirs, Meriel Buchanan describes the physical appearance of the fifteen-year-old Olga at an imperial ball in 1910: "That evening . . . she wore a pale-pink chiffon dress of almost classical simplicity, a silver ribbon was bound round her golden hair, which was parted in the middle, and her only jewels were a string of pearls round her slender neck. She had not the regular features, the almost mystical beauty of her sister, Tatiana Nikolaievna, but with her rather tip-tilted nose, her wide laughing mouth, her sparkling blue eyes, she had a charm, a freshness, an enchanting exuberance that made her irresistible."

In November 1911 Olga turned sixteen, which was considered the coming of age for Russian aristocratic girls. Every young girl impatiently awaited this first "grown-up" ball, her coming out to the world. A grand dinner and gala party was taking place on that day at the palace in Livadia in the Crimea, to celebrate Olga's birthday.

Those who received the following invitation considered it a great honor: "Their Imperial Majesties invite [You] to dinner and a dancing party to be held on Thursday November 3rd, at 6:45 in the evening, at the Livadia Palace." Dress for the occasion was strictly regulated: "Military cavaliers in frock coat with epaulets. . . . Civilians in evening dress with white tie."

General Alexander Spiridovich, the Chief of Secret Personal Police in charge of protecting Nicholas II and his immediate family from 1905 until 1914, described the gala: "Dinner was served on small tables. Many candles, silver, flowers. At the round table in the center were seated Their Majesties, Grand Dukes Nicholas Nikolaevich, Pierre Nikolaevich, Alexander Mikhailovich, George Mikhailovich, with their wives, and the Minister of the Court. The star of the party, Olga Nikolaevna, in a pink dress, for the first time with her hair in a chignon, presided over the table. Her escort was N. P. Sablin. Still a young girl, very naïve, she often asked her escort what she should do. . . . All flushed in the face, charming in her pink dress, Olga Nikolaevna literally beamed with joy at the great favor accorded to her regiment [the 9th Hussar regiment of Elizavetgrad, of which Olga was the chief]. They congratulated her and kissed her hand."

Unlike her sister Maria, Olga did not often talk about wanting a husband and lots of children. However, it is evident from her diaries that she was a very romantic girl, who often idealized the young men she developed crushes on. During the winter of 1913–14, after Olga turned eighteen, several royal young men were considered as potential husbands for her. Among them were her cousin Grand Duke Dmitri; Prince Arthur of Connaught; the Duke of Leuchtenberg; and even briefly Edward, the Prince of Wales.

When the Crown Prince and Princess of Romania visited Russia, they brought along their eldest son Prince Karol, and everyone anxiously awaited the announcement of his and Olga's engagement. The Romanian royals stayed at Tsarskoe Selo for several days, but in the end nothing came of this venture. The grand duchess and the prince evidently were not romantically attracted. Olga mentioned this visit briefly in her diary, and the impression we get is disinterest at best.

The two respective royal families did not, however, completely give up on the idea of the marriage, and that summer Olga and her parents boarded the *Standart* and sailed to Constanta, Romania. Olga was too smart not to figure out the reason for this journey. She mentioned to Pierre Gilliard that she was aware that everyone was hoping for the Romanian engagement, but that her father had promised her that she would not be forced into a marriage that was distasteful to her.

Diplomatically, Olga never actually said that she did not like the Romanian prince as a potential husband. Instead, she insisted that the reason she did not want this marriage was because she did not wish to leave her beloved Russia or change her nationality, as she would be forced to do if she married Prince Karol. The idea of the Romanian engagement was eventually abandoned, and as Russia entered the world war later that summer, there was no more talk about it.

The coming of war marked a great change in Olga's life. Instead of the social activities and balls of peacetime, Olga and Tatiana joined their mother in training as military nurses or "Sisters of Mercy." Working together in their contribution to the Russian war effort no doubt strengthened the strong sisterly "We 2" bond between Olga and Tatiana.

After August 1914, Olga's diaries are full of her impressions and thoughts about the infirmary that was set up at the Catherine Palace in Tsarskoe Selo, which was the sisters' own hospital, and about the patients themselves. The two younger sisters, Maria and Anastasia, had their own separate infirmary; however, they were too young to officially train as Sisters of Mercy.

In the twilight of 1916, events turned progressively more dismal for Olga and her family. Meriel Buchanan recalled: "Spending her days working in the hospital, butting [caring] for the wounded, caring for her brother who had fallen ill again after a visit to Headquarters, the Grand Duchess Olga saw her mother daily more exhausted, more strained, more unhappy, and eventually overwhelmed with grief when Rasputin was murdered on December 16, 1916."

Olga may have been the only one of her siblings who understood at least some of the implications of what was happening in her country. According to Buchanan, Olga "was keenly aware of the growing menace and dangers of the situation. 'Why has the feeling in the country changed against my father?' she asked a lady-in-waiting, and then the latter replied that to explain that it would be necessary to go back to the reign of her grandfather who had countermanded all the progressive, constitutional plans of her great-grandfather Alexander II. Olga was silent and pensive, not entirely satisfied perhaps, wondering if there were not more ominous reasons for the unrest and ferment that she sensed rather than knew about, but which filled her with a growing anxiety."

Olga stopped writing in her diary in March 1917, just as the frightening events of the Russian revolution began to intensify. There was no explanation or even a hint of why she chose to stop writing. Later she did write a number of letters to her relatives and friends from exile, but never again did she write another line in her diaries, eventually destroying at least one of them. It is unclear why she chose to burn part of her diaries, just as her two youngest sisters did, and why she left the rest of the volumes intact. Perhaps it was because most of her diaries were packed away in chests and suitcases after the family was moved to Siberia and the Urals, and she had no access to them.

Olga's life ended before her twenty-third birthday, a life that by many accounts was full of potential. What kind of a woman would she have become if she had been given the opportunity to live out her natural life? No one will ever know. What is left behind are the diaries and letters of Grand Duchess Olga Nikolaevna Romanova, as well as the reflections of those who knew her. These provide a revealing glimpse into the character of this sensitive and intelligent young woman, who happened to be the eldest daughter of the last tsar of Russia.

1914

The year 1914 started out as any other for the imperial family and for Russia, and they had no way of knowing that this would be the year when everything would change. Anna Vyrubova, a close friend of Empress Alexandra, writes in her memoirs: "1914, the year that became fatal for our poor motherland and for almost everyone in the entire world, started out peacefully and calmly." At the beginning of the summer the family went to Livadia, Crimea, for their usual Black Sea shore holiday.

In August, Russia entered World War I and life as they knew it would never be the same. To contribute to the war effort, Olga, her sister Tatiana, and her mother Empress Alexandra trained as Sisters of Mercy. Part of the Grand (Catherine) Palace at Tsarskoe Selo was turned into a military infirmary where the two girls and their mother worked, changing dressings, assisting at surgeries, cleaning instruments, distributing medications, reading to patients, and helping them write letters. The girls were also involved in various charitable organizations and events to raise money for war veterans and their families. For the first time Olga was exposed to the darker side of life. The family was also physically apart for extended periods, which had not occurred before. Olga and her siblings missed their father, who was now often away at Stavka (military headquarters) in Mogilev. They corresponded with him regularly and looked forward to his letters and telegrams. Olga turned nineteen in November 1914.

—

Yr. 1914

Tuesday, 7th January.
Went on Vetka [train] to meet Aunt Ella.[1] Breakfasted in the library with Papa, Mama. Unc. Boris and Unc. Georgiy.[2] During the day we 3 with Papa skied down the hill by the White Tower. Mama at the bottom. Lots of fun. Spoke on the telephone with Aunt Olga. At 10 1/2 to bed. It was boring. Papa in his [rooms] reading.

Wednesday, August [sic] 26th.[3]
Today is Grandpa's[4] birthday. Had breakfast with Grandma[5] and Aunt Ksenia[6] and Unc. Sandro.[7] From there, rode to Krondshtadt, to the Archeological Committee. Watched some interesting digs. Ran into Sh.[8] on Nevsky.[9] Returned by 4 o'clock for tea and dinner with Papa and Mama. Papa and T. played a little.

1st March, Saturday. ~~29th February.~~ [sic]
Lessons. At 12 hrs 20 min. we 2 with Papa rode to have breakfast at Grandma's. Ladies-in-waiting were there too. At 2 o'clock to the Fortress.[10] *Panikhida*[11] for Great-grandfather[12]

1. Grand Duchess Elizaveta Feodorovna (1864–1918), formerly Princess Ella of Hesse.
2. Grand Duke Boris Vladimirovich (1877–1943), son of Grand Duke Vladimir and Grand Duchess Maria Pavlovna the Elder and Nicholas's first cousin. Grand Duke Georgiy Konstantinovich was son of Grand Duke Konstantin.
3. Here Olga erroneously wrote "August" instead of "February."
4. Alexander III (1845–1894), Nicholas's father.
5. Dowager Empress Maria Fedorovna (1847–1928), Nicholas's mother.
6. Grand Duchess Ksenia Alexandrovna (1875–1960), Nicholas's sister.
7. Grand Duke Alexander Mikhailovich (1866–1933), husband of Grand Duchess Ksenia Aleksandrovna.
8. Pavel Voronov: One of the officers, Olga's crush.
9. Nevsky Prospekt, the main thoroughfare of St. Petersburg.
10. Sts. Peter and Paul Fortress.
11. Orthodox prayer for the dead.
12. Tsar Alexander II (1818–1881), Nicholas's grandfather, known as "Tsar-Liberator" because he freed the serfs. Assassinated by a terrorist.

and Great-grandmother.[13] The entire family was there. [It's] warm in the sun. Skied down the hill. Papa worked on the ice. Mama went out in a little sleigh. She was very tired bec.[ause] in church, [illegible] was not long and she received [people]. Tea and dinner with Papa and Mama. Went to *vsenoshnaya* [vespers]. In the evening looked at pictures and sketches of churches in Yaroslavl and Rostov. Sat with Mama until 11 o'clock. Papa read a lot in his [room].

Saturday. 22nd March.

At 10 hrs. 20 min. we 2 [referring to herself and Tatiana] with Papa. Aunt Missy, Nando and Karol[14] went to the Winter Pal.[ace],[15] where they watched the parade of new recruits from the windows. Long, but nice. Had breakfast at Grandma's, with Mama, Aunt Olga[16] Aunt Ksenia, Unc. Sandro and Aunt Marie.[17] From there went to Grandpa's[18] museum. The Romanians left . . . and [we] had tea at home.

Wednesday. 26th March.

Aunt Ella came [onto the train] at 9 3/4 o'clock in Moscow, and stayed until 91/4 until Kursk. Sat with Mama all day.

Holy Christ's Resurrection. 6th April.

At 11 o'clock, *Khristovaniye*[19] downstairs and Mama gave out eggs. During the day to Anya's[20] with Mama. In the evening

13. Empress Maria Alexandrovna (1824–1880), Nicholas's grandmother, first wife of Alexander II.
14. Romanian royal family.
15. Imperial palace in St. Petersburg, currently the Hermitage.
16. Grand Duchess Olga Alexandrovna (1882–1960), Nicholas II's younger sister.
17. Grand Duchess Marie Pavlovna the Elder (1854–1920), Grand Duke Vladimir Alexandrovich's wife.
18. Presumably refers to the Russian Museum, founded in 1895 by the new emperor Nicholas II to commemorate his father, Alexander III.
19. Orthodox Easter service.
20. Anna Vyrubova (1884–1964), close friend of Empress Alexandra.

went to [see] Aunt Mavra[21] . . . and returned for tea time. Anya [came] for dinner too. . . . In the evening sat with Mama.

Saturday. 14th June.
Moleben[22] at 9 1/2 for M.'s birthday (did our hair) and at 10 o'cl. we 4 [refers to herself and her three sisters: Tatiana, Maria, and Anastasia] with Papa, Mama, Aunt Olga, Unc. Kyril,[23] Aunt Ducky[24] and George[25] headed to "Alexandria" in Kronstadt,[26] English squadron. Looked at the "Lion," a colossal thing. Very classy. It was raining, but warm. Had breakfast [illegible] then departed, Went on the "New Zealand" but did not stay long.[27] Tea with Papa and Mama. Dinner too and with Unc. Kyril and Dmitri.[28]

Saturday. 19th July.
Talked with [name in code]. Tea with Papa and Mama and breakfast with Ioann,[29] dinner also, and with Dmitri and Aunt Olga. During the day took a walk with Papa. After *vsenoshnaya* it was announced that the German swine have declared war on us. God help us. So difficult.

---

21. Grand Duchess Elisaveta Mavrikevna, née Princess of Saxen-Altenburg, wife of Konstantin Konstantinovich (KR).
22. Supplicatory prayer service used within the Orthodox Church in honor of Jesus Christ, the Mother of God, a feast, or a particular saint or martyr.
23. Grand Duke Kyril Vladimirovich (1876–1938), Nicholas II's cousin.
24. Grand Duchess Victoria Melita, Kyril Vladimirovich's wife, first cousin of Empress Alexandra.
25. Grand Duke George Mikhailovich (1862–1919), first cousin to Nicholas II's father, Alexander III.
26. Kronstadt, located on Kotlin Island, nineteen miles west of St. Petersburg, near the head of the Gulf of Finland, was St. Petersburg's main seaport and naval base.
27. The British warships HMS *Lion* and HMS *New Zealand* arrived in Russia. Some members of the Russian imperial family, including Olga, came on board as part of this visit.
28. Grand Duke Dmitri Pavlovich (1891–1941), son of Grand Duke Pavel Alexandrovich, first cousin to Nicholas II, was involved in Rasputin's murder.
29. Prince Ioann Konstantonovich (1886–1918), son of Konstantin Konstantinovich (KR).

—

From the memoirs of Anna Vyrubova:

The days before the war was declared were awful; I saw and felt how the Empress is trying to make a dangerous decision. I played tennis with the children daily; returning I would see the Tsar pale and upset. . . , At this time a telegram from Rasputin in Siberia arrived, where he was in bed wounded, [he was] begging the Tsar: "do not start a war, with the war it will be the end of Russia and of Themselves and that every last man will be killed." The Emperor was annoyed by this telegram, and he paid no attention to it.

—

Thursday. 24th July.
We 2 slept with Mama, went on to Alexandria and picked up Aunts Victoria[30] and Ella. Returned for breakfast and left before dinner.

Passed by dear Yalta. Overcast and rainy. During the day sat at home, sewed. Rode our bicycles. Later at 6 o'clock ended up at Anya's with her 3 charming nieces. Aunt Olga came for dinner with [illegible] and talked. Austria declared war on us. Bastards.

—

From the memoirs of Anna Vyrubova:

Their Majesties' Petersburg arrival on the day of declaration of war confirmed the Tsar's prediction that war will wake up patriotic spirit in the people. Thousands of people everywhere with national flags, and the Tsar's portraits. The singing of the hymn "Lord save Thou people." Not one of the residents of the capital stayed home that day. Their

30. Princess Victoria of Battenburg, Alexandra's sister.

Majesties arrived in Petersburg via the sea. They walked from the boat to the Palace, surrounded by the people, who cheered them. We barely got through to the Palace; on the stairs, in the halls, [were] crowds of officers all over and various persons who had access to the Court. It is hard to imagine what happened when Their Majesties came out. In the Nikolaevsky Hall, after molebna, the Tsar addressed all present with a speech. At first his voice shook from nervousness, but later he started to speak confidently and with inspiration and ended with the words: "That he will not end the war until every last enemy is driven out of the Russian land." In response there was a deafening "Hurrah"; sounds of admiration and love; the military crowded around the Tsar, waved their hats and yelled so [loudly] that it seemed that the windows in walls shook. . . Their Majesties slowly returned and the crowd, ignoring court etiquette, ran to them; the ladies and the soldiers kissed their hands, shoulders, Empress's dress. She glanced at me when she passed by and I saw that her eyes were full of tears. When they came into the Malachite room, the Grand Dukes ran over to ask the Tsar to show himself on the balcony. When they saw him, the entire ocean of people on the Palace Square, all as one got down on their knees in front of him. Thousands of flags bent down, hymns were sang, prayers. . . Everyone was crying. . . Among these feelings of endless love and loyalty began the war.

They moved to Tsarskoe Selo where the Empress, forgetting her illnesses, set up a special evacuation point, which included 85 infirmaries at Tsarskoe Selo, Pavlovsk, Peterhof, Lug, Sablin, and other locations.

———

Thursday. 21st August.
After *Znamenie*[31] [went] to change dressings. I have 3 new [patients] wounded in the arm. Later sat with Mama's offi-

31. Chapel in Tsarskoe Selo.

cers. [Name in code] was there for breakfast, for dinner too. Anya [came] for tea. It's sunny—and good news: [we] took Lvov and Galich. Thank God. The Serbs are also winning over those dirty scoundrels. Before tea rode our bicycles along with Papa in a kayak. To bed at 10 o'cl. Gr.[igori] Yef.[imovich][32] came by.

Friday, September 19.
Tea with Uncle Kostya[33] and Aunt Mavra. Around 4 o'clock took a walk with Papa. Mama too. 15 degrees,[34] raining and cold, sunny in the morning. Grigori Yefimovich came by in the evening. Aleksei's knee and arm hurt. [He is] lying down.

—

Letters from Olga to Nicholas II:
20 September.
My golden Papa, may the Lord God keep you. Although it is so hard to part from you, I am glad that you are going. When the army sees you it will be easier for them to fight and it will be nice for you to see them. So, farewell, sunny-Papa. I love you so so much and kiss you.
Your always loyal and loving daughter— Olga Romanova.

22 September.
My dear golden Papa!
Thank you very very much for your telegram which made us all happy. I am so happy that the darling is with you.[35] And so nice about our victory. Thank God. All the wounded came alive, and the little flags on the maps were moved forward, i.e. to the West. We three are sitting in Mama's lilac

32. Grigori Yefimovich Rasputin (1872–1916), spiritual advisor to the imperial couple. Murdered by Felix Yusupov and others.
33. Grand Duke Konstantin Konstantinovich, Nicholas's second cousin, known as KR.
34. All temperatures are in degrees Celsius.
35. Aleksei went to Stavka with his father.

[mauve] room and writing to you, while Mama is already in bed. She has a very bad headache. She regrets awfully that she cannot write to you. She kisses you affectionately and wishes you a good night.

Nastasia and I walked a bit today and went to the warehouse. There were about 6 ladies working [there], and Madame Sapozhnikova, [who is] incredibly fat, and most of the time [she] did everything wrong, so that Trina had to redo everything. At 6 o'clock Tatiana and I went to Anya's. Grigori and Zina were there, not Anya's but the one who comes to him often, very charming, and finally Princess Gedroitz. She decided not to give the lecture since Mama was not there, and [we] went to listen to Grigori. He poured tea for us and told us a lot of interesting things. He said that the strong rains helped us, and other good stuff. The weather is clear, but very cold—only 1 degree of warmth. "The Evening Flyer" [newspaper] just came. It says it came to the active army. Could that be true? A. I don't know why I wrote this letter ["A"].

Well, goodbye, sunny-Papa. Sleep well and dream of many good things. Forgive me for my silly letter. May God keep you. I love you very much and kiss you. I am with you with my entire soul.

Always Your daughter
Elisavetgradetz[36]
Big regards [from] A.A.

—

Saturday, September 27th.
Had tea at Irina's[37] then stopped by at Grandma's and Aunt Ksenia's. After 7 o'clock got home—[it is] very cold.

36. Olga was the chief of the Elizavetgrad Regiment.
37. Irina Alexandrovna (1895–1970), daughter of Grand Duchess Ksenia.

Monday, October 13th.
Breakfast and dinner with Gavril, and later we 2 changed dressings again until 3:30. Thank God, the news is good, a lot of weapons and still advancing.

—

Letter from Olga to Nicholas II:
21 October.
My Golden Papa!
You left and it feels so empty; but we did not stay home a lot. Until 5.30 we were at our infirmary. From 2 o'clock changed the dressings in the Grand House [Catherine Palace infirmary], then sat with our officers. [I] gave your regards to Iedegarov, and he was frightfully happy, and asked me several times how you said this, and was awfully happy. He says that today he is the happiest man on earth. We rode to the lower church of the Grand infirmary (the palace one). On Sunday we will have the good fortune to be present at its consecration. The style is Ancient Byzantium, very pretty and white.

At 6 o'clock 2 officers from the Red Cross and 1 from Krat, 93rd regiment, came to say goodbye to Mama. They are returning to their regiments. After that we went to Marie's and Nastasia's infirmary. They have a lot of seriously wounded, one poor chap died last night, another is dying and is in a coma.

And over there is a brave dragoon of the 16th Tver regiment—he has a broken arm, he is cheerful and tells [stories] charmingly. He himself is a Don Cossack. He was sent somewhere with a report, and he alone encountered 30 of the enemy, he got surrounded of course, but he was so excellent with his rapier that he was able to break through and flee. They chased him of course, but he says that no one can catch up to a Russian horse. So there it is. Right now we are going to eat dinner, later I will host a fun committee meeting, but for now I will end.

Continuing on the morning of the 22nd. Today it is overcast, but not very cold. I am rushing to finish this as there is someone waiting. We just came back from Petrograd where we collected charity. Reviewed our 2 trains of Madam Sukhmlinova's and . . . [illegible]. . . They are set up pretty well. Huge dressings change room. They are leaving in 2 days. Well, goodbye, Papa darling my dear.

May the Lord be with you. I love you so affectionately, a kiss and regards to Nikolai Pavlovich.[38]
Your loyal Elizavetgradetz.

—

Wednesday, October 22nd.
Tea, dinner, breakfast with Mama. Overcast. Papa arrived in Minsk. Again with his departure victories began, thank the Lord.

—

Letters from Olga to Nicholas II:
23 October.
Sunny-Papa!

What a great happiness our victories are. All our wounded [patients] came alive, and Your darling Nizhegorodtzi[39] Iedegarov and Chakhava are eager to return. Especially the latter, he does not care where he goes, as long as he can chop someone up. Our trip to Luga was rather successful. We left at 1:30 o'clock during the day and arrived there in 2 hours and 5 minutes. Mama and I sat in the coach with two horses. We rode for a long time and finally ended up in Svetelka.

38. Admiral Nikolai Pavlovich Sablin, former commander in chief of the Russian army.
39. Meaning from Nizhny Novgorod.

Tolstaya and V. P. Schneider almost fainted when they saw Mama, and kept cackling with joy. . . I think I [just] wrote a bunch of silliness but the sisters are annoying me with their endless chatter. And now Aleksei came in, in his blue robe, to say goodbye to Mama. He sat down on the floor and is eating dark crackers, he kisses you. Mama is reading agency telegrams to us, the rest of them are knitting, while I am writing. We are having sunny weather, but cool. Not a lot of snow. Well, goodbye, my golden beloved Papa. May the Lord be with you. I kiss you very very affectionately and please send regards to Nikolai Pavlovich. How is he?
Your loyal Elisavetgradetz.

26 October.
My golden Papa!

I feel so badly that I did not write to you yesterday, but I had absolutely no free time. The church consecration went well. It was very hot and all the relatives were there. Uncle Kostya with his wife Elena, Kostya, Igor and Georgiy, the old Aunt Olga and Uncle Pavel,[40] and all of them were standing with us in the little room near the altar. From there we went to see our wounded [patients] for a minute. Almost all of them were in the church too. The weather is overcast today, but warm. Right now we are going with Mama to the Invalid house, or some other infirmary. Your Nizhegorodzti look really appetizing in their blue and mauve pants. . . .

Well, goodbye, my darling Papa. May Christ be with you. I kiss you very affectionately and regards to Nikolai Pavlovich,
Your loyal Elisavetgradetz.

---

40. Grand Duke Pavel Alexandrovich (1860–1919), Nicholas's uncle, brother of Tsar Alexander III, and father of Dmitri Pavlovich and Marie Pavlovna (the younger).

—

Sunday, 26th October.
Rode to the consecration of the cave cathedral of the Palace
Infirmary. All the wounded were there. Iedegarov (the
Muslim) and K., stopped by their place from there.
Breakfast, tea, dinner with Mama. During the day went to
Liazonozonovs, the wounded officers, ours too, and to the
Red Cross. Snow, warmer in the evening [minus] 2 [degrees]
of frost. At 6 o'clock rode with Aleksei to our
[people/friends]. Chahava talked a lot. Regrettably, Iedegarov
and K. are in the city. [Had] a cold. Papa telegraphed from
Brest.

—

Letter from Olga to Nicholas II:
21st November.
On the train between Tsarskoe Selo and Luga.
My golden Papa!
Had no chance at all to write to you earlier. Now going to
bed. Nyuta is brushing my hair. Today Iedegarov left us,
which is very sad. Next week to the regiment, but for now to
the city to see his wife. . . .

Continuing on the 22nd.
At first it was really boring—endless hymns and [they]
showed [us] photos on canvas: You, all of us and the allied
Royalty. Then the singing. The best were the balalaikas and
singers from the railroad regiment. It was all so nice—the
audience cheered with delight. There were a lot of wounded
and they were cheered. . . Arrived in Vilna at 10 o'clock 15
minutes in the morning. . . From there, in a nice closed
motorcar driven by a soldier, went to the cathedral to [see]
the holy relics of 3 saints. . . . At the end of this headed to the

infirmary—of the Polish nobility. It was a nice set up, in a huge bright hall, on the pews where the officers sat. From there went to [see] the miracle-working icon above the gates but all was for naught since we did not [get to] kiss the image, and Mama walked up the steep ladder for nothing. Unexpectedly ran into Pavel Nikolaevich in a coach, which was very pleasant.

Then went to a 4 story infirmary, which you have been to too. . . Took photos there with many nurses and officers. . . now going to Kovno. The weather is nice, 2 degrees of warmth. I hope that you will be able to read my terrible, shaky handwriting. . . We were proudly ridden around in a lighted motorcar. In the last one, we went around to see more than 40 prisoners of war and 1 officer. I did not converse with them. With us is Nastenka, since Isa has fever and stomach ache, and she was put to bed for 3 days. . . Went to *Obednya* today. Now are riding the Loman train.
May Christ be with you, Papa my darling.
I kiss you very very affectionately.
Your loyal *Elisavetgradetz*.
Regards to Nikolai Pavlovich.

Continuing on the 23rd in Tsarskoe Selo.
In Landvorovo, where the headquarters of general Renekampf was located, had *moleben* and rounds of medical locations. Among us were the wounded Germans. A very appetizing looking black doctor Ganin. . . . At one of the stations, after dinner they brought the medical train, in heated cars 11 people each. They are all energetic and very charming. Got ready for bed—talked a lot.

—

Wednesday. 31st December.
Znamenie, then to the infirmary for dressing changes. Kostya had breakfast, [then we] went to the Red Cross at the Grand Palace. In the evening, 6 [deg. of frost.] Papa received Alexandro-Georgeyevski cross[41] of the 3rd level. I am so happy. In the evening *moleben*. Lord save us for the new year . . . and help Papa—Amen.

41. Military imperial award for bravery in combat.

1915

As 1915 dawned, Russia entered the second year of World War I. The year began dramatically: on January 2 Anna Vyrubova was critically injured in a train crash, and Grigori Rasputin appeared to save her life, which reinforced the family's confidence in his healing abilities. Olga, Tatiana, and their mother continued working at the infirmary alongside the other Sisters of Mercy. Even on Sundays, holidays, and their own birthdays, the girls and their mother were busy tending to the soldiers, not shunning such mundane tasks as darning socks and pillowcases. Most of all Olga seemed to enjoy spending time with and getting to know the patients themselves—young wounded officers—and she did her best to make their physical and emotional pain more tolerable. It is clear from her diaries that she grew rather attached to some of the patients. Although Olga managed to have some occasional fun with her new infirmary friends, gone were her innocent and happy days aboard the family yacht. No longer would Olga get to swim in the Black Sea during vacations in Livadia, and never again would she attend another ball. Her new world now mostly revolved around Russia's war with Germany and Austria. This year proved disastrous for Russia's war involvement, with an inexperienced Nicholas II acting as direct commander of the army, leaving the ambitious but incapable Alexandra in charge of the government. Perhaps to hold on to some sense of stability, Olga continued some of her favorite "normal" pastimes, which included riding her bicycle, playing the piano and board games, and regularly attending church services.

Princess V. I. Gedroitz was a medical doctor at the imperial infirmary who worked closely with Olga, Tatiana, and

Alexandra. In her memoir, she wrote down heartfelt, if perhaps overly reverent, impressions of Olga and her mother and sister:

> The first three months from the start of the war there were around three thousand [wounded] people in the Tsarskoe Selo region who were distributed among various infirmaries in Tsarskoe Selo. . . .
>
> The Tsaritsa of the Russian Land, Empress Alexandra Feodorovna, thought of all, and felt and understood with her heart. She came to us with her August daughters Olga and Tatiana Nikolaevnas. Very simply, came to show us a great example of love, entering our ranks as simple pupils, then nurses, not demanding any special privileges, contributing to [their] work not dilatancy, but deep consideration, showing the example of respect to the existing rules, strict in our fortunate infirmaries. She came and told us: "Teach us, like everyone else," and it was easy to teach [them] because "their hearts were burning" with spirited love to close ones, and they did not demand any special regard, or privilege, but learning. . .
>
> They lived with us through the most wonderful, soul-shaking gamut of human suffering, did not avoid even one hardship. . . . Their hearts did not flee from anything! And when at the end of the training the August Sisters of Mercy were given exams along with everyone else, and our operating rooms were enriched with three knowledgeable surgical nurses, and Russia—with three hearts which were eternally tied to it by the chain of suffering, a chain which cannot be broken or forgotten.
>
> Their high example was not singular; it destroyed the walls of etiquette, fortunes and ranks. . . Everyone went with the same passion, the same love, same words: "teach us like everyone else."

—

Yr. 1915

Thursday. 1st January.
Holy God help us. Went to *obednya*. K.[1] also. Ate all together. Walked with Al.[eksei] on the hill. . . T.[atiana], A.[nastasia] and Papa walked too. He received diplomats and the suite. Went to the Grand [Catherine] Palace. In the evening, not much. Mama feels tolerable all the time.

Friday. 2nd January.
Znamenie, dressing changes. Darling Sh. was there. He was sad for some reason. Ended up at a concert at the Grand Palace. K. was there. After dinner ended up at our infirmary with Mama. There was a train crash. [Anya] was hurt very badly, poor thing, but is conscious. K. came by. Gr.[igori] Yef.[imovich] came over. [He] stayed all night, [illegible] with her [Anya]. Left after 12 o'cl. Papa was there.

Wednesday, 8th January.
Anya received the most darling letter from Iedegarov from Tiflis. "Znamenie." Changed bandages for Sychev, Gumanuk, and Emelyanov, of 21st Sibirsky Shooters Regiment of Mama's, he is very sweet, left shoulder is fractured. In the Grand Palace, appendicitis. Uncle Boris and Ioann had breakfast. From 3 until 5 were there again with Mama. Papa came too. Anya feels better, she feels calmer. Stood with K. and others, talked, etc. At 7 o'clock Anastasia and I rode to the Grand Palace. Ioann had breakfast, I mean, had dinner. In the evening went to our [people/friends]. With Nurse Grekova cleaned instruments for tomorrow's

1. Vladimir Kiknadze: "K" of the 3rd Regiment of his Imperial Majesty. A Georgian and favorite of Grand Duchess Tatiana.

surgery. After 11 o'clock to bed. Save us, oh Lord. [Minus] 4 [degrees] of frost.

Monday. 2nd February.
Went to meet darling Papa. Saw [coded name].[2] Returned to the infirmary around 10 o'cl. Changed dressings. . . Sat with K. for a little while, and others. At 11 1/2 to the grotto church.[3] Mama also. During the day took a walk with her and Papa in the garden. Sat with Anya for a long time. She is better and [is] cheerful. After 11 to bed—so nice that Papa is home. At 10:30 to *obednya*, Maria and I with Papa. Aleksei later. . . . Later, Papa worked while we returned on a donkey and at 4 o'clock rode to the Grand Palace. Saw K. through a keyhole. [He] was hiding somewhere. . . .

Monday. 9th February.
Prince Yusupov had breakfast. He [just] returned from abroad. During the day rode with Mama and [we] were endlessly photographed at the Grand Palace. After tea, rode with Isa.[4] Nice—wet snow. . .

Tuesday. 10th February.
At 3 o'clock went to Pavlovsk with Mama, Uncle Kostya [KR] is very ill. Sat with Tatiana,[5] later the children came over—Elena[6] was not there. . . .

Saturday. 21st February.
At 9 1/2 went to *Znamenie* with Mama. . . Anya is better, thank God. Changed dressings. . . At 1 hr. 20 min. to the

2. A code Olga uses throughout the diaries to refer to one of her crushes.
3. Chapel in the cellar of Feodorovsky Cathedral.
4. Baroness Sophie Buxhoeveden (1884–1956), lady-in-waiting to Alexandra.
5. Tatiana Konstantinovna, KR's daughter and Olga's cousin.
6. KR's daughter-in-law.

city. I have a major committee [meeting]. Then went to pick up T. at Irina's and Felix's. Aunt Ksenia and Andrei[7] were there. Wonderfully sunny—but cold. The entire family went to *vsenoshnaya*. In the evening went to visit Anya. [name in code] [talked] with K. on the telephone. Papa was there too.

Friday. 27th February.
Our darling Yemelianov was transferred to Matveyevski infirmary, [I feel] so restless and sad. . . 25 deg. in the evening. [text in code][8]

   K. was there. Awfully difficult in general. Ate all together—during the day we 4[9] took a walk. Later to the Grand Palace with Mama and at 4 o'cl. to Anya's, [name in code] was there. In the evening *kolorito*[10] with Mama. At 10 o'cl. she and Papa [went] to Anya's. 2 deg.

—

Letters from Olga to Nicholas II:
5 March.
My golden Papa!
   I am writing to you while sitting on the floor of Mama's sitting room. She and Marie are playing *kolorito*—Tatiana is knitting a stocking, and the little one is already upstairs. We were in Petrograd today. I had the pleasure to preside over the big committee [meeting] for 2 hours. It was such fun. . . From there we went to Irina's for Tatiana. She and Aunt Ksenia were visiting there, while Felix [was] a "typical civilian," wearing all brown, was walking around the room, dig-

7. Grand Duke Andrei Vladimirovich (1879–1956), son of Grand Duke Vladimir.
8. Written in code or shorthand, which Olga does in her diary occasionally, presumably for privacy. Antonina Voronskaya has decoded this text to read: [He?] felt sick, and so ashamed, [I] cannot look anyone in the eyes and himself.
9. Olga and her three sisters.
10. A game.

ging into various drawers with magazines and in essence doing nothing; he makes a rather unpleasant impression, such an idle man during such time. These days it is rather cold, but the sun is shining and it even warms up. It is really boring in the city with such weather. Oh, yesterday N. V. Plevitzkaya came to the charity committee—she is very appetizing looking. She wants to do her first concert in some theater in support of my committee. So lovely!

We were present during two surgeries today at the Big house, and during this time they were bringing out the body of Grabovoy and the music played "Kol' slaven," this reminded me so much of the lowering of the flag on the yacht, and then the funeral march. In the city we met commander Zelenetsky, riding a coach [wearing] a simple overcoat, probably he was going to visit "The Bird" so he did not even notice us. Pass this on to Nikolai Pavlovich, he will probably be happy, and please send regards to him. Recently a blind *strannitza*[11] who has the light of the Lord's Tomb [*sic*]. Do you remember when we saw her in Peterhof? She is so cozy, she prays and reads out loud the longest passages by heart. Well, I will end now. May the Lord keep you, my dear Papa. I love you very very much and kiss you. Always Your loyal *Elisavetgradetz*.

5 April.
Papa, my darling dear!

So you ended up at Stavka. I hope that you will be able to escape from there soon. Such a shame that you weren't able to work on the ice today. The water was level with the little bridge, so it was really easy to drag the ice bits for us 4 and Nagorny. We kept on closing the barriers (were afraid that

11. Female religious pilgrim.

the water will overflow)—and threw the pieces over two boards, so the flooding was rather successful, it even sprayed through the cracks in the rocks. Occasionally we took a rest on small stools, which we brought from home. Aleksei rode over in his motor with little Sergei and the handsome Aleksei, who never even came out [of the motor]—they are too afraid for them to catch cold etc. *Obednya* was successful in all aspects—the soldiers sang, very well, but in the end they got confused and started to sing *litia*, for which the *Batushka* was not ready at all, and instead of "Christ has Risen" they sang "Eternal Remembrance." . . . Aleks. Konstant. was at the meeting. . . . We went to the infirmary in the morning. . . . During the day [we] went to the Grand Palace, but everyone was gathered there to hear a concert, so we were a little embarrassed and hurried to leave, and went to Marie's and Nastasia's infirmary. They were playing various games there with their patients. Had tea at Anya's with Kozhevnikov and Rodionov. Later Aleksei came over and we played "*dobchiski-bobchinski*" and "post office," like in Kharaks[12]—remember? They are leaving on Tuesday.

Nastaska and Shvybzik[13] kiss you and are going to bed. Tatiana is sitting nearby and reading, while Mama is playing *kolorito* with Marie, Ortipo [Tatiana's pet dog] is sleeping by her feet. Right now it is exactly 5 of 9 o'clock. Well, I will be ending now. May Lord keep you, my golden Papa. I love you so much and kiss you.
Your Elisavetgradetz. Send regards to Nikolai Pavlovich.

11 April.
Papa, my jewel! So good that you were able to go to all these places. It must have been so interesting. All is the same with

12. Crimean villa of one of the grand dukes.
13. Anastasia's nickname, meaning "the imp" in German.

us. The weather is average—sunny, then rained, or rather drizzled. Today the wife of Your Erivanetz Purtzeladze stopped by Sonya Orbeliani's[14] with her son—Andrusha—a charming boy with large gray eyes and golden hair. He is 2 years old. His father is a prisoner of war in Shtralzunde, he wrote to his wife a few times, but of course was not able to tell her much. . . . Right now there is a big commotion. Ortipo is scampering around the room, while the little Shvybzik is squealing. Mama and Marie are playing *kolorito* as usual, and take turns winning. Anya tends to show up at Mama's daily, around 12 o'clock. Zhuk, the nurse's aide of the reserve regiment, pushes her in a wheelchair and assists her on crutches. We haven't been [working] on ice for a while. In the last few days we rode around in various *charabancs*[15] and navigated them ourselves. This is not a bad activity, especially during nice weather. We went to *vsenoshnaya* and it was lights out until 8 o'clock—very pleasant. . . . Viktor Erastovich and Demenkov [came] to tea. Marie of course is as happy as a pug.[16] Mama received an awfully nice telegram from the Georgian regiment. They were all so happy and touched by your regard. . . .

After the dressings we went to the Big house for surgeries. Today they cut the little *zhid*[17] Mazik, who screamed before they even touched him, intending to go to sleep.

Well, I think this is all the news.

May the Lord keep you, Papa my darling.

I love you very much and kiss you.

Your Elisavetgradetz.

Regards to Nikolai Pavlovich and congratulate him on the 16th [his birthday].

14. Georgian Princess Sonia Orbeliani, friend of the imperial family.
15. Horse-drawn vehicle.
16. Marie was happy to see her crush Nikolai Dmitrievich Demenkov.
17. A derogatory term for a Jewish person. Olga was a product of her environment, and contemporary Russia was extremely anti-Semitic, especially in aristocratic circles.

17 April.

Papa my dear, my darling!

I hope that this is my last letter and you will soon return. It is disgusting what is going on in *Okhta*. Rezin went there today, and Uncle Alek spent the entire day there. Tatiana is playing "*Fibikha*" on the piano for our listening pleasure—which is very boring. Mama and Marie are playing *kolorito* of course. We three rode horses for the second time during the day. Marie on your Gardeman, and I on Regent. I was riding him again in Peterhof at our parade. . . Nastasia rode around Pavlovsk in a *charabanc*. We ran into cross-eyed Vera who was riding around in a semi-covered landau with her governess. The weather was cold and no less windy. We have not worked on the ice for a while. Everything was cleared until the little bridge, but occasionally a thin layer of ice covers it (not sure if I wrote this word correctly). . . .

On Wednesday we went to the city as usual. I received more than 2,000 rubles. Nice, right? And before that we went to one of my infirmaries "The Merchants of *Sennaya* Square," which has 50 beds. . . . From there we went to see Countess Hendrikova. Poor thing, she looks awful, in every sense of the word. . . . The sisters wrote to you repeatedly about last Sunday at Anya's. We were there exactly from 5 until 8, it was such fun—Nikolai Dmitrievich was really funny, he was in charge of all the games, and at the end told us 2 jokes. . . Aleksei just came here. He will be praying with Mama now. He kisses you.

It's time for me to end. I kiss you my angel Papa and love you so much. May the Lord keep you.

Your loyal *Elisavetgradetz*. Regards to Nikolai Pavlovich, Chemodurov,[18] darling Kotov and Litvinov.

---

18. Nicholas's valet, who was killed with the family in Ekaterinburg.

Just spoke with Sergei Mikhailovich on the telephone, and he gave me the details about *Okhta*. 82 critically wounded, 7 of them died, they found 97 corpses and 57 men are missing. 3 workshops burned down completely, no damage to the army, thank God, as all the bullets, grenades etc., are safe in other warehouses. Forgive me that I write of such bad things.

19 April.
Papa, my darling!

In honor of Easter Sunday we visited 2 infirmaries again. . . . Drenteln came here with a box of medals and we gave them out. Everyone was very grateful. There are some critically [wounded], and the recuperating ones all want to return to the army, and smile charmingly when they are asked about it. The weather is overcast and cool. Mama is still lying down on the balcony.

This morning before *obednya* in the grotto church, Sergeant Kuznetzov was converted from old belief to Orthodoxy. It was rather solemn and nice. When his feet had to be anointed, they brought him a chair and he pulled off his shoes. *Batushka* was rejoicing and gave a short instructional sermon. At the end of it all my godson Panfil kissed my left cheek. Such a darling. During *obednya* he confessed and held a lit candle in his hands the entire time. Mama and Aleksei were in the church too. They came for "*Veruyu*" ["I Believe"] and stayed until the end. Right now we are sitting at Mama's after dinner. After 5 o'clock we headed to Anya's, where Alexander Konstantinovich, Viktor Erastovich, and Nikolai Dmitrievich already were. We had tea together. At 6 o'clock Aleksei came and we started playing. At first *dobchinski-bobchinski*, then charades. It was a lot of fun and funny, especially when Viktor Erastovich played with Nastasia. Nikolai Dmitrievich helped both parties. Aleksei too, as it was not fun for him to guess, but he still played.

Madam Yanova sent us a lot of flowers from Livadia. What joy it was. Lilac, wisteria, golden rain, Judas tree, 1 peony etc. and also lilac irises, which have opened since yesterday.

Right now it's snowing and everything is already white— which is not necessary at all, but at least it's not so cold. Forgive me for such appalling handwriting. Tomorrow we will see the Voronovs, also at Anya's. They came to visit for a few days. Semenov is also here. His older sister, who was at the Grand Palace, reported this to me. During the day yesterday Tatiana Konstantinovna [KR's daughter] was driving the charabanc herself. She hit something, turned over and now is in bed with torn ligaments. Well, I think that's it for Tsarskoe Selo news.

Well, until we meet soon. Papa, my jewel. May the Lord keep you. I kiss you very very affectionately.
Your loyal Elisavetgradetz.

—

Thursday. 23rd April.
At 10 1/3 *obednya* in honor of Mama's Day of the Angel.[19] Grandma, Aunt Ksenia, Uncle Pavel and Dmitri had breakfast. Beautiful weather—took a walk with Papa, later he kayaked, and we on *Gatchinka* and on the motor. Mama sat on the balcony. In the evening Papa played billiards with Dmitri. Mama and we [were] nearby. Lord save us.

—

Letter from Olga to Nicholas II:
30 April.
Hello my dear Papa!
Tatiana is sending you these postcards. The weather turned really awful, and it seems like it's already autumn, and

19. The name day is the feast day of one's namesake saint.

this is really unnecessary. At least today the snow is all gone. I am afraid that all the flowers will freeze, especially the cowslip which started to blossom. Grandma sent me and Tatiana the Red Cross step 1 medal yesterday, so this made us pompous. Yesterday we went to the Silayevs with her and spent our time cozily. All the girls were so lovely. We took them around the entire house, to the attic, the kitchen etc. to their mother's chagrin. She, meaning Silayev's wife, received two letters from 2 former Erivantzy who ended up in different regiments during the mobilization, and they are begging to somehow be transferred back to their own regiment. They were in Your group in Livadia, lovely simple people, they heard that Silayev got a regiment and are eager to return even more, [they] are saying that they are ready to die, but in their own regiment. So she told me about this since she doesn't know what to tell them, and I decided to ask you. They are all terribly happy with their new regiment commander, one of our patients wrote that they could not ask for better . . . and thank God for that. The other day, after 7 o'clock in the evening, I rode with Aleksei in a carriage, just the two of us. It was very cold and wet, but it was fine, we pleasantly rode by all the usual favorite roads, past the 3rd Shooter regiment barracks, through Zakahrievskaya St, where Irina's house was pointed out [to us], and so forth. There were not many patients left, most of them departed on Anya's train to Yevpatoria. Well, Papa darling, it's time for me to end. May God keep you.

I kiss you affectionately and love you.

Your Elisavetgradetz

—

Monday. 4th May.

Bandaged 3 [wounded] with fractures. Ate all together. At 3

1/2 to a concert at A.'s and M.'s infirmary. In the evening Gr.[igori] Yef.[imovich] came over. At 10 o'cl. *moleben.* [image to be inserted] was there—and at 10 1/2 saw darling Papa off. Raining. 2 deg.

—

Letter from Olga to Nicholas II:
5 May.
Papa, my darling!

I congratulate you from the heart and kiss you affectionately. Right now it is already 5 o'clock, and Mama and Tatiana have not returned from the city. They left me, since I continue to cough intensely and so forth. Mama changed Vodyanoi's dressing this morning at the infirmary. She will send you the paper on which he wrote himself. He has an awfully wonderful face.

The weather is windy, but sunny. I am in a big hurry as I may be late.
May the Lord be with you, my golden Papa.
Your loyal *Elisavetgradetz.*
I kiss you 1000000 times.

—

Friday, 8th May.
At a train station in Vitebsk. Arrived here at 8.30—unloaded the motor cars. At 9 o'clock headed to the cathedral. They performed a short *moleben* and from there [we] went to four infirmaries. The weather is warm, everything is in greenery. At one of the infirmaries we took photos with the wounded in the garden.

Around 12 o'clock came back here. Mama had breakfast in a chaise lounge, as she was tired. . . At 3 o'clock we went to the warehouse at first, where they produce some sort of medicines etc., and send them to active army, from there [went] to 2 large infirmaries.

Later we saw a work shop at the governor's house and had something to drink, Artzimovich's [governor] sister gave us a treat. From there we went to one more infirmary and came back here at 6.20, headed to a medical train which just arrived. Walked through it, altogether [there were] 15 cars, did not enter the caboose.

All the wounded were exclusively from the infantry division. Left at exactly 7 o'clock. Marvelous evening and sunset, passing by beautiful areas, lakes. Had supper with everyone. Mama is in her [car], tired and has a backache. Walked at the Ezreshe station. Papa is staying at Stavka for a few more days. Admiral Essen[20] died yesterday—horrible loss. Going to bed now.

—

Letter from Olga to Nicholas II:
9 May.
Papa-sunny!

Until now couldn't get around to writing you. We are sitting after dinner in Mama's lilac room. She and Tatiana are playing some game, Marie is playing *Izhe Kheruvymi* on the piano and hitting a lot of wrong notes. Nastaska is writing something. Ortipo was chasing the little machine and Trupp's shoe buckle and has now calmed down. It was so nice at the *vsenoshnaya*. The entire church was full of greenery. The birches bloomed a little and were everywhere, upstairs and downstairs in the corners. The weather, although sunny, but after Vitebsk is very cool. It was so nice there. Everything covered in greenery, bird-cherry trees are blossoming, the

20. Admiral N. O. von Essen, the Russian Baltic fleet commander, died in May 1915 from pneumonia.

fruit trees too. I approve of Governor Artzimov. He is very considerate of Mama not getting overtired and so forth. And in the city and everywhere there is always excellent order. But only too many *zhids*. When we departed, the guards stood at attention. Some of them were dressed in hussar uniforms, very similar to mine. . . It was so cozy to sleep in the train, but only a little too cool, since [we] woke up early. . . I think that's all. Tell the admiral that Olya returned. She got tan, feels better, but is still very nervous and cries easily. The rest of the ladies-in-waiting are unchanged.

It was so awfully sad, the death of admiral Essen. Remember, when he used to come on the whaleboat with a "Thank God" and a briefcase with a report for you? I am not going to write about the grenade explosion,[21] it is such villainy.

I am ending now. May the Lord keep you, my jewel Papa darling. I love you very very much and kiss you.

Your loyal Elisavetgradetz. Regards to Nikolai Pavlovich— and from Nastaska to Viktor Erastovich and from me too.

—

Saturday, 9th May.
Nikolai Pavlovich and Emelianov's name days. At 9 o'clock arrived [at Tsarskoe Selo], around 10 o'clock to *Znamenie*, to the infirmary to Anya. . . . Vodyanoi of the 150th Tamansk regiment had his tongue cut out and part of his ears. . . . Drups has a wound in [his] stomach, of the 224th Yukhnovsky regiment [*sic*]. Stood in the hallway with the others.

Fresh, sunny, 3 degrees in the evening. During the day [rode] in the charabanc with Maria. Tatiana [rode] with

21. Olga is referring to an unknown, unrelated incident here.

Anastasia. Papa is staying a few more days. At 6 o'clock [went] to the graveyard with Mama. Visited Gr.[igori] Efim.[ovich]. Later to *vsenoshnaya*. Nice, everything is in greenery. Around 11 o'clock to bed. Sonia Orbeliani had breakfast.

Sunday. 31st May.
Went to *obednya*. Aunt Ducky had breakfast. Sunny, warm and breezy. Walked with Papa, Mama in a wheelchair (we on bicycles) to Bablovo. At 4 1/2 to Anya's. M., A., darling Sh., Z. and Ivan put on a small play. The first rehearsal was awfully funny. In the evening T., M. and I went with Papa to [illegible], to the village Suzy and then home through Bablovo. Beautiful sunset but cold. In the evening Gr. Yef. came by, [he was] cheerful.

Tuesday. 2nd June.
At 2 1/2 went to the graveyard with Mama. . . . Picked up T. at 3 o'cl. and went to the Grand Palace, upstairs to Mama's warehouse (surgical department). At 4 hrs 20 min, we 2 with Papa to the city. Darling Sh. met us. Had tea at Grandma's. Came home at 7 o'cl. At 9 o'cl. went to Pavlovsk for the *panikhida* for poor Uncle Kostya, he passed away at 6 1/2. Sat with all of them and for a little while with Elena, who did not feel well and [was] lying down [illegible] on the couch. Around 11 o'cl. to bed. Lord save us.

—

Letters from Olga to Nicholas II:
11th June.
Papa-sunny!
It is so lonesome now that you left. The weather is marvelous today. I am sitting near the tennis court on the grass

under a tree, *pikhta* I think, and enjoying the warmth. The sisters got stuck back there somewhere. Mama and Anya are on the balcony. We were just at the Grand Palace. Almost all the patients are in the garden, and fortunately not that many visitors. . . .

Last evening I had a committee; it lasted about a half hour, Volodya Volkonsky chaired, very short and clear, even funny it was, because he read so quickly. Right now it is 4 o'clock—the bell has tolled. After tea we plan on squeezing the children at the nanny school, since we have not been there for a while. The soldiers are singing from afar, birds are chirping and it's cozy in general.

I hope that you will not miss Stavka too much. Did Savitsky (the Cossack) get handsomer? Mosquitoes are starting to sting and exasperate. Sorry for the silly letter, but somehow hard to write. I kiss you, Papa my darling, a thousand times. May Christ be with you.
Your loyal Elisavetgradetz.
Regards to Nikolai Pavlovich.

16 June.
Darling, my dear Papa!
So how are you? We are all [fine], thank God. The weather is warmer finally, but evenings are still damp—so that after 9 o'clock Mama prays with Aleksei and we go inside, a shame, it's still light out but in here it feels like winter. Today we worked a lot and long in the warehouse. It was quite fun, and we rolled a large amount of bandages. The wife and the very lovely daughter of Count Dmitri Ivanovich Tolstoy and others worked with us. The exhibition is still very successful and rather interesting. The most pretty infirmary department is Marie's and Nastasia's. All our work was sold, so we are working again. Mama and the little one are especially trying

hard. At 6 o'clock Tatiana went horseback riding, and I listened to the rehearsal of the play at Anya's house. Now everything is going really well, and even Anya is happy with the lovely actors who really are trying hard. Aunt Olga wrote that poor Daphne [a pet dog] died and she and Emilia Ivanovna cried a lot, burying him under the flowerbed. Did not get to play tennis. Papa, darling, I want to see you so much. Regards to Nikolai Pavlovich and Lozinsky. Such bore to go to the city tomorrow for charity and to some infirmary. And what an awful incident with poor Kazbek. It's already the third son. Sorry for the silly letter, it all came all confusing and foolish. Farewell, Papa-sunny. May God keep you. I kiss you very very affectionately and love you so.
Your loyal Elisavetgradetz.

21 June.
My darling Papa!
   I am awfully happy that you are coming back soon. I am sitting with Mama on the balcony after breakfast. Isa just came out and sat in the armchair which I planned [to use] myself. The sisters are going to the Grand Palace and the infirmary, and I don't think are too happy about it. When they return, we will go to ours. They have arranged a croquet game and we will play. Aleksei and his endless suite are going to Ropsha, but will return at 6 o'clock, in order to go to Anya's. Alexander Konstantinovich went to the Caucasus to buy a horse and so forth, so on Sundays it is now less cozy, although still fun. By the way, Father Kedrinski has been hit by a trolley, and his left leg was amputated—poor thing, especially unfortunate for a priest. On Wednesday Tatiana and I had tea at Grandmother's on Yelagin and returned on the motor for the first time. Rode for an hour and five minutes, since there is road work in the city and very backed up.

Irina and Felix had tea with us yesterday. They said that Andrusha was dressed as a page with spurs—and was rather embarrassed at first. Today Kostya is coming over. He is leaving to the regiment in a few days. Isa continues sitting and talking a lot. Our *Yerivantzy*[22] are recovering way too fast and tomorrow the best of them is returning to the regiment, which is very sad. During all these months we had 15 officers as patients from their regiment. We met the former *nizhne-gorodetz*[23] Kusov at Anya's. He was in the Moscow Dragun regiment for 4 years already. We felt right at home with him immediately, and he did even more, and he talked about masses of things. Last night he visited us, count and countess Grabbe, Nini Voikova and Emma Fredericks. Alya sang, and it was rather cozy. Isa finally left and I will be ending. May God keep you, Papa, my jewel. I kiss you very very affectionately and love you. Your loyal Elisavetgradetz.

Regards to Nikolai Pavlovich. Tell him that he is a pig, because he did not even write once. I started twice but it didn't come out and tore it up.

25 June.
My golden Papa!
Didn't get the chance to write you with today's *feld-yeger*,[24] since there was no time. We went to the Grand palace infirmary today with Aleksei, and it was amazingly boring and lame, as we and the sisters stood by one tree, and the patients by another, and could not part for a long time. After that we played a game of tennis for the first time since Your departure. Four nets all different and I lost them all. The weather was wonderful, and the sun was very strong, so we are slow-

22. From Yerevan.
23. From Nizhny Novgorod.
24. *Feld-yeger* literally means field huntsman.

ly getting tan, and the evenings are so cool, so that it's cold to sit outside in a dress. Here on the balcony it got very cozy ever since Mama acquired the new wicker furniture made by the invalids, and the two lamps stay lit. Now the tea table was brought in, and Galkin is fixedly shoving Anya's wheelchair under the table. Papa darling, I think about you so much during these anxious days. God willing, everything will soon pass and things will become "more lighthearted," as Grigori always says. Oh yeah! We 4, Isa, Kira and Vilchkovsky went to *Kolpin* yesterday. It is much warmer there than here, and really beautiful near the river. We went to six infirmaries and a church where the image of Nikolai Chudotvorets [Miracle Worker, one of Russia's main saints] is. There were rather a lot of workers and among engineer-mechanics [was] Solovov—remember him from the yacht, and then on "*Abrek*." I apologize for the ink smudge I just made. Kolenkin is at our infirmary—his left ear is infected, but he is better. He arrived to the Alexandrisky regiment for only a week, but everyone loved him very much and he is revving to return.

Well, I am ending now. May He keep you, Papa, my angel.

I kiss you and love you very very much.

Your loyal Elisavetgradetz.

Regards to Nikolai Pavlovich.

—

Sunday. 28th June.

During the day ate on the balcony with A., M. and T. At 5 o'cl. went to meet darling Papa. I am so happy that he is here. Until 10 o'cl. sat on the balcony—raining heavily. . . . Lord save us.

Wednesday. 1st July.
We 2 to *Znamenie* and to the infirmary. Changed dressings. .
. . Sat with the Yerevantzy[25]—it was so cozy. At 2 1/2 we 2 to
the city to charities and after that to Yelagin—Papa too. Had
tea with Grandma and Aunt Ksenia in the garden. Vasya was
there. Warm, but not very. Returned at 7 1/2. Had dinner on
the balcony. . . . Anya came over. Mama is feeling fair. At 11
hrs 10 min. to bed.

Saturday. 11th July. [Olga's name day]
We 2 and Al. to the infirmary. From there to *Znamenie*.
Changed dressings. . . At 12 1/2 had *moleben* for me.
Grandma had breakfast. Sat on the balcony with Mama and
wrote telegrams. Very warm—14 deg. In the evening went to
vsenoshnaya. Later, we 3 with Papa and Mama to Pavlovsk. Sat
on the balcony with T., Aunt Olga, Mavra, Ioannchik . . .
and Elena. Came home at 11 o'cl. Save us, Holy Lord.

—

From the memoirs of V. I. Chebotareva:[26]
Zalivsky's surgery on the 21st went very well. Tatiana
Nikolaevna handed over the silk, and Olga Nikolaevna the
instruments, I—the equipment. In the evening, we came
again to clean the instruments, all sat terribly crowded.
Opened the windows ourselves, dragged over the silk ourselves. O[lga] Nikolaevna once again said "Mama sends her
regards especially to you, Valentina Ivanovna. It is so nice
here, if there was no war, we would not have known you, so
strange, isn't it?" Scrubbed thoroughly with soap, alcohol,
prepared instruments and put them into the closet ourselves.

---

25. Officers from Yerevan, Georgia.
26. Valentina Ivanova Chebotareva was a fellow nurse at the royal infirmary and friend
to the grand duchesses.

The officers were surprised "But you have attendants, why ruin your hands!"

26 July.

The Empress and the grand duchesses started working in August [1914]. At first they were so distant! [We] kissed hands, greeted the grand duchesses, and that was the end of it. Vera Ignatievna gave lectures in their room for a half hour, and Anna Alexandrovna was always there, then [we] went to do the dressings: grand duchesses—the soldiers, the Empress and Anna Alexandrovna [Vyrubova]—the officers.

—

Saturday. 22nd August.
Papa, Mama and Aleksei were in the city, receiving [members] of the Duma. Breakfast on the balcony with Nikolai Pavlovich, marvelous weather. Caught 39 bees. During the day walked with Papa and Nikolai Pavlovich. Mama on a cart in Bablovo. Spoke to Mitya[27] on the telephone. Tea in the playroom. Anastasia was downstairs in the evening. . . Nikolai Pavlovich and Anya had dinner. At 10 o'clock went to the train station to see off darling Papa. Lord help and save him on this new difficult journey as the Commander-in-Chief[28]. Mama was tired from everything and these difficult times. [We] went to bed right away. . . .

—

Letters from Olga to Nicholas II:
24 August.
Papa, my priceless jewel!

27. Dmitri Shakh-Bagov, ensign of His Majesty's Guard's Yerevan 13th Guards Grenadier.
28. Nicholas recently appointed himself commander-in-chief of the army instead of Grand Duke Nikolai Nikolaevich.

Your evening telegram made everyone really happy. May
the Lord help you. . . . Shvybzik [Anastasia] had breakfast
with us but [she] sat at a separate table in the sun. There were
a lot less wasps. At 9 o'clock we went to *Obednya* in the grotto church. The little *batushka*[29] Anfis did the service. There
were many appetizing looking children [their height] below
the knee, took the host, and it took a lot of restraint for me
not to grab and squeeze them. After this, we went to do
dressings at the infirmary, dressed everyone really fast since
there weren't too many patients, and went to play croquet.
There was a lot of laughter and arguments, as I don't think
that there was any way to play more dishonestly than we did.
The rest of the non-ambulatory patients sat in wheelchairs
and on benches, like in a theater, and laughed hysterically.
Aleksei asked me to send you a kiss and tell you that he will
write about Irina Tolstaya. We had cozy time at Anya's, with
her and Rita Khitrovo.[30] She grew even more and is awfully
lovely. In the evening we took a ride with Mama in a half
open motor around the boulevard and a little farther, it was
very warm and dark. Oh yeah, I was at the Grand palace during the day. Half of the patients were in the garden, and
when it started to rain, they carted them into a large tent,
where they lived nicely for a while. Anya had breakfast at
Countess Paley's[31]. . . Alya's husband came for a few days. He
got tan and more buff, but looks weak in a *chekesska*. He is
being transferred to the 3rd *Ulan* regiment, it's really not necessary, right? Anya read Volodya Paley's[32] lovely poetry to us,
they were copied down by his mother. And this morning, as
usual, went to the infirmary. At the end of the dressings

29. Father/priest.
30. Margarita Khitrovo (1895–1952), lady-in-waiting and friend of Olga.
31. Countess Olga Paley, morganatic wife of Grand Duke Pavel Alexandrovich and
mother of Prince Vladimir Paley.
32. Prince Vladimir Pavlovich Paley (1897–1918), son of Grand Duke Pavel
Alexandrovich and his morganatic wife Olga Paley and first cousin to Nicholas II.

Mama came, to everyone's joy. In the meantime, the weather is awful. It's raining, cool and foggy. We had breakfast upstairs in the playroom, as Aleksei's arm hurts a bit. He regrets that he cannot write to you today. We sat there for an hour—Mr. Gilliard read something to Aleksei, and before and after breakfast he showed us his magic lantern.[33] Right now I am sitting in Mama's lilac [mauve] room by the window. We just came down. She was planning on resting but was reminded that Ordin and Apraksin are waiting, and she was forced to go and receive them. Upstairs in the red room the tuner is sitting at the piano and I am rather sick of him, banging out one note.

Well, Papa my dear, I am ending now.

May Christ be with you. Regards to Kolya, and I kiss you very very affectionately.

Your loyal Elisavetgradetz.

27 August.

Papa, my darling!

I am writing to you in Mama's lilac room, in Your comfortable easy chair. She just left. We have dinner in the playroom these days, and it is so cozy. The weather today, although clear, is cold. During the day we rode in 2 equipages to the *Pavlovsk* forest. It was so nice there, reminded me of *Belovezh*, and also *Shkheri*, as we found a few cowberries and bilberries. Uncle Pavel had tea with us and later talked with Mama "in private," while we headed to Tatiana's [Konstantinovna] who arrived for a few days from the village and is living in *Strelna*, and spent the day in *Pavlovsk* today. She looks a little better, although still very thin. We saw Your goddaughter Ekaterina in her grandma's arms, she is very darling. I am not going to talk about Vsevolod. Kostya sat there the entire time being a

---

33. Movie projector.

pest. Georgii too [KR's sons], he had a cold and was intruding into conversation the entire time, which was tiresome. Afterwards went to *vsenoshnaya* in the upper church, and the *batushka* gave a long but good sermon. It's a shame that more people can't hear him. Yesterday we 2 went to the city. At first went to see the charity warehouse for Tatiana's refugees. . . . From there headed to the Winter Palace, Tatiana to a committee, and I to charities. Received a lot of money, more than 2,000 rubles, but there were not a lot of people. Volkonsky was very pleasant, said a lot of interesting things. Countess Karlova was the "birthday girl" and we all forgot to congratulate her, of course. Had tea on Yelagin with Grandma and Aunt Ksenia. Aunt Ksenia had a cold and did not feel well, and was pale, while Grandma, thank God, is fine. She was happy about the good news. . . . Irina [Alexandrovna] had a stomach ache and was lying down [in bed] for a few days. Anya just came and sat down in your easy chair and I migrated next to the piano. During the day we went to the Grand palace. The patients there are 4 young ensigns from *Preobrazhensk*. They are all together and their rooms are called "Children's," since they are acting naughty like small children, for which they get chastised sometimes, but what else have the poor things to do. Now it's time to go to bed, therefore I will be ending, Papa my dear, everyone was awfully happy about Your letter to Mama. She read some excerpts to us, and we squeezed you in our minds and loved you an awful much, Papa our little jewel. Continuing on the 28th. We are sitting on the balcony having tea. The weather is exceptionally nice. . . During the day we rode again and at one of the farm stands in Pavlovsk bought two wonderful jars of raspberry and bilberry preserves. Aleksei is also spending the entire day in the garden. During the day, before our walk, we went to the Christening of ensign Kobb's son. Marie was the godmother, and former *Ulan* Yakovlev (commandant of her train) [was] the godfather. His eldest boy, whose Christening was last year with Mama, was very lovely. Nikolai Dmitrievich was the duty officer, so Marie was fussing around a lot and yelling on the balcony. At Anya's we saw the wife and daughters[34] of Gregori Yefimovich. She is so nice and cozy. Papa, darling, it's time for me to end. Right now we are going to the *vsenoshnaya* and the general confession—I am asking Your forgiveness.

May the Lord keep and help you.

I kiss you affectionately and warmly, my dear Papa, kiss you the same way I love You.

Your loyal Elisavetgradetz.

—

Sunday. 30th August.

Sonia Orbeliani[35] had breakfast on the balcony, tea there too. During the day rode around, I with Mama and the sisters in the back. Aleksei [went] to Peterghof. Went to the graveyard of the wounded and Count Nirod. Spoke with Sh[vedov] on the telephone, his name day. Lord save us. Papa telegraphed. Dinner in the playroom. Mama is [feeling] fine, thank God. . . . Spoke with Mitya, he is sad for some reason, poor little thing. . . . Lord help us.

—

Letters from Olga to Nicholas II:

1 September.

My Dear Papa!

I just saw an officer from my regiment. He was wounded and had a contusion and in a few days is already returning to

34. Rasputin's wife, Paraskovia, and daughters Varvara (Varya) and Maria (Matriona).
35. Princess Sonia Orbeliani, Georgian friend of the imperial family.

the regiment. Now we are going to ride with Mama and Anya in 2 different equipages. Tatiana has a Russian lesson. Marie and Nastasia are tormenting Petr Vasilyevich[36] all the way. This morning we had surgery for that contused officer whom you saw in Tiflis, and he asked for a transfer here. Remember him? But his head doesn't shake anymore, although his left arm and leg are not functional. So, it's 6 o'clock here. We had a good ride during the day, rode around all the *Pavlovsk* streets, completely unfamiliar. There are so may cozy houses. Just got a letter from Uncle Sandro. He writes that he saw you, and I am envious of him. The mood of everyone there is very good, and in general apparently he is satisfied with everything. Papa, darling. I will end now— silly letter.

May the Lord help and keep you.

I kiss you affectionately and warmly.

Your loyal Elisavetgradetz.

I finally saw dear Alexander Konstantinovich at Anya's last night.

5 September.

Papa my darling!

The weather turned horrible. Pouring for the third day in row, and rather cold. Marie, Anastasia and I are sitting at home. Just went to the Grand palace. There were a lot of new wounded and contused patients. . . Before that we went to Lianozovoy's infirmary. An officer from *Leib-guards* of the Petrograd regiment is a patient there. And another, poor thing, very contused, who used to be our patient, had hysterics last night, and he poor thing cried a lot and for long time and stuttered. And before that we stopped by the infirmary

36. The imperial children's Russian tutor.

which doesn't exist anymore, and it came off rather lame. We often used to pass by it and never got around to going in and today got around to it and there was nothing there instead of the infirmary, except a girl who was cleaning the room. Mama and Tatiana are in the city. Yesterday there was a very successful concert at Marie's and Anastasia's infirmary. . . The soldiers were so happy and clapped enthusiastically. Aleksei continues to run into Irina Tolstaya daily. Kostya[37] killed a young elk yesterday and is planning on giving me the head, after stuffing it. I am not too happy about this. First of all, why kill such a young one, without antlers? Then, what I am going to do with it? Well, Papa my jewel, I wish you all the best. I kiss you affectionately. May the Lord be with you. Your Elisavetgradetz.

—

Saturday. 12th September.
Looked at a [photo] album with Mitya[38] and others. Stopped by [to see] everyone and [sat] on the balcony with Mitya for a minute. Ate with Mama. During the day [went] with Maria and Anastasia to their infirmary, later we 4 took a walk. Raining and damp. . . Aleksei had a mud [bath]. Papa telegraphed. Spoke with Mitya. . . .

—

Letter from Grand Duchess Olga Alexandrovna to her niece:
15 September, Kiev 1915.
    My very own darling Olga, writing to you while sitting on a wide window sill on the 3rd floor of our gymnasium—Hospital. It's so hot that it's wonderful, but unfortunately there is little time to enjoy this, either dressings from 9

37. Konstantin Konstantinovich.
38. Dmitri Shakh-Bagov.

o'cl.–3 o'cl., and after dinner before tea surgeries—and in the evening one is already tired and it's pleasant to just go to one's room and stretch one's legs and read until supper. I was in the sanitarium for the mentally disturbed officers—this is in the Sosnov woods—"Svyatoshino" and very quiet, cozy and nice there. But am awfully sad and feel such pity for these wretched young people—ruined and suffering for the rest of their lives. I myself started to sleep badly and don't feel well sometimes, don't know why. The sisters[39] tormented me—one of them was rude and did not want to listen. . .

—

Friday. 2nd October.
. . . For a long time sat on a window sill with darling Mitya, later in a chair, he on a table, I knitted. He has [temp of] 37.1, fine in the evening, [wearing] a thick robe. Ate with Mama. Papa telegraphed. Saw the 21st corps. Rode with Mama. Cold. Went to the grave yard. In the evening talked with Mitya. . . Mama was tired, since we were at the Grand Palace for prayer services and went around to [see] everyone.

—

From the memoirs of V. I. Chebotareva:
24 October.
These days the Empress comes over, so charming and affectionate and tender, [she] spoke with me so affectionately and graciously. Turns out that she eats neither meat nor fish out of principle: "About ten-eleven years ago [I] was in Sarov and decided not to eat any more animal flesh, and then the doctors found that this is necessary for my health." [She] sat for a long time in the dining room with her work. One of the

39. The Sisters of Mercy nurses.

grand duchesses was playing ping-pong, the other checkers, some read, some chattered, all so uncomplicated and cozy. The Empress said to Varvara Afanasievna: "Look at how much fun the little ones are having, how this simple life lets us relax. . . the large gatherings, higher society—brrrr! I return to my own [place] completely broken down. I have to force myself to speak, to see people who I know well are against me, are working against me. . . The court, their intrigues, all this cruelty, how torturous and tiresome it all is. Recently I was finally relieved from some of this, and even that was only when there was proof. When I distance myself from this society, and arrange my life the way I like it, then they say: "she is a haughty person," they criticize those whom I love, but in order to be able to judge they need to know all the details. Often I know what kind of person is in front of me; it's enough for me to glance at him once to understand whether he can be trusted or not."

Poor, wretched woman. . . This is how I always saw her—herself pure and good, wholesome and simple. . . she cannot believe in Grigori's[40] filth. The result—enemies in the upper echelon and distrust from the lower.

. . . Today Tatiana Nikolaevna initially came alone: "I come here as to my second home," and indeed she was so charming and cozy. Ran with me into the kitchen, where we were preparing the dressings. The Empress laughed and said that Tatiana is like a nice pet dog, got so used to it. Poor Olga Nikolaevna is really sick—developed severe anemia, they put her to bed for a week, but with permission to come to the infirmary for a half hour for the arsenic injections.[41]

—

40. Rasputin.
41. Arsenic injections were used to treat various disorders by contemporary doctors.

Letters from Olga to Nicholas II:
29 October.
Papa my darling!

It was probably really interesting in *Revel*. All is the same with us. The weather is very pleasant, 4 degrees of warmth. We sledded with Trina,[42] and now sit with Mama. Anya and Alya and the eldest girl, whom we squeezed a little, were there. Marie and Nastasia went to their infirmary and when they returned they will have a massive amount to say as usual. Tonight I will have the joy to sit on a committee, although a small one, but long. Such fun. At the infirmary they injected me with arsenic, after which I intensely taught the patients to play *kosti* [a game], like you, but they of course do not understand anything and are playing their own way with no rhyme or reason or scores. This letter is rather uninteresting, and I apologize for that. Now it's time to go have tea.
I kiss you affectionately, my Papa. Also Aleksei.
May the Lord keep you.
Your loyal Elisavetgradetz.
Regards to Nikolai Pavlovich and others.

7 November.
My dear darling Papa!

We just had breakfast with Mama, and she is already receiving Vilchakovsky. Tatiana is having a lesson. Marie and Nastasia went to their infirmary, and at 3 o'clock we will go riding with Nastenka.[43] Although there is a lot of snow we are still riding in a carriage. I went to the infirmary twice already and did not do anything but sit with them. But they are still

42. Catherine Adolfovna Schneider, lady-in-waiting to Alexandra.
43. Countess Anastasia Henrikova (1887–1918), lady-in-waiting to Alexandra and friend of the imperial family who followed them into exile and was murdered by the revolutionaries.

making me lie down again, and Evgeni Sergeyevich[44] injects me with arsenic daily, from which I stink like garlic a little, which is even less pleasant. I can't report anything more interesting, I received my milk brother[45] yesterday, who volunteered for my regiment. He is nice enough, but does not have a lot of bearing yet, and we embarrassed each other a little.

We often run into strolling Countess Paley in Pavlovsk, in her own pleasant company. The two little princes less often. So Papa, darling, I am ending now. Today saw Count Gelovani who returned from Evpatoria. He looks good, gained weight.

I kiss you and Aleksei affectionately.

May God keep you.

Your Elisavetgradetz.

—

From the memoirs of V. I. Chebotareva:
4 December.
And how can we know what kind of drama Olga Nikolaevna lived through. Why is she melting, losing weight, looking pale: in love with Shakh-Bagov? A little but not seriously. The general atmosphere that lords over [us] nowadays does not inspire peace. As soon as dressings end, Tatiana Nikolaevna goes to do the injection, then sits down with K. The latter is constantly restless, first sits by the piano, playing something with one finger, chats a lot and fervently with the charming child. Varvara Afanasiyvna is appalled, what if Naryshkina walks in on this scene, Madame Zizi, she would die. Shakh-Bagov has fever, is in bed. Olga Nikolaevna sits by his bed constantly. The other couple also moved there, yes-

44. Dr. Evgeni Botkin (1865–1918), court physician who went into exile with the imperial family and was murdered along with them.
45. Child of one's wet nurse.

terday [they] sat by the bed and looked at a photo album. K. is being so coy. Tatiana Nikolaevna's small dear child's face cannot hide a thing, [it looks] pink, excited. Isn't this closeness, the physical contact harmful[?]. I feel scared. The others are jealous, angry, and I imagine they spread all sorts of [rumors] throughout the city and later beyond. Vera Ignatievna is sending K. to Evpatoria—thank God. Away from sin. Vera Ignatievna told me that Shakh-Bagov, while intoxicated, displayed Olga Nikolaevna's letters. That's all we need! Those poor children!

———

From the memoirs of I. Belyaev:

The grand duchess Olga Nikolaevna had her very own "protégé": the sick young ensign from Yerevan—Shakh-Bagov, very sweet and shy like a girl. It was obvious that he was utterly in love with his nurse. His cheeks burned with a bright flame whenever he looked at Olga Nikolaevna.

———

From the memoirs of V. I. Chebotareva:
7 December.

Yesterday at 6 in the evening the grand duchesses called Varvara Afanasievna, and were so affectionate and pleasant [to her] as usual. Meanwhile, Tatiana Nikolaevna asked "What time do you think mother went to bed? 8 in the morning!—Evidently she spent the entire night by Aleksei Nikolaevich's bed.—After a half hour she got up and went to church."

The grand duchesses changed in front of Varvara Afanasievna, and chose their jewels. Olga said: "Only such a shame that no one can have the pleasure of seeing me, only Papa!" complete absence of brashness. One, two—[her] hairdo is ready (no hairdo), [she] did not even glance in the mirror. . . . Anastasia was not allowed to go to dinner, had to go to bed early, which was why she had dinner alone with the nanny in her giant lonely "upstairs." Before Varvara Afanasievna visited them—Olga was—sick,—Nyuta brought a gramophone disk "Goodbye Lou-Lou." . . . So sad, these poor children live in a golden cage.

—

Letter from Olga to Nicholas II:
12 December.
Tsarskoe Selo.
My dear darling Papa!
It was so cozy to sleep on the train for 2 nights, and especially this one, right here at the station, and not at home, I was able to fall asleep before the stop. From Chudov to Novgorod, where we are changing the route to a new one. And the train is moving very quietly the whole time. The weather was not very cold, it snowed sometimes, but foggy. The town is small and because of that is quaint. . . Stood for a 2 hour *obednya* in Sofyisky cathedral, eparchiral of course and went around to look at various relics with open dried up hands and kissed them! How elegantly I have described this. The bishop Arseniy gave a long sermon as a greeting. Bishop Aleksei assisted him with the service. He imagined himself to be handsome and made appropriate grimaces, benevolently-buttery. From there he dragged us to the bishop's house, dragged us through all the chambers and halls. At one point Mama sat down in a chair for a 1/2 a minute and then was dragged again. At the end of the building they had an infirmary. Went around it very quickly and descended down into antiquities depository.

Many lovely old icons, 2 male nurses who picked Mama up on a ramp will eventually get watches as a reward.

Ioannchik, Andrusha[46] and the governor had breakfast with us. They rode with us everywhere. Islavin was great, did not allow [anyone] to delay us anywhere, gathered the wounded from the many small infirmaries into a large one, etc. At 2 o'clock [we] went again: at first to some small city infirmary, to the Desyatensky nunnery. There was something like a *molebna* and [saw] a St. Varvara[47] relic. The nuns crowded around as usual. Igumenia dragged Mama into her cell for 1 1/2 minutes they also hauled in the bishops. They also went with us everywhere. We walked from there through a courtyard to the *staritza*[48] Maria's cell. It was very narrow and dark and only one small candle was lit, which was extinguished immediately, then they lit something like a kerosene lamp without a lampshade, and the nun shed a tear and held it. The *staritza* was lying on a wooden cot behind some sort of mended curtain full of holes. She was wearing large iron chains. Her arms, so thin and dark, [are] almost relics. She looks 107 years old. Her hair [is] very very sparse, in disarray and her entire face [is] covered in wrinkles. Her eyes are light and clear. She gave each of us an icon and a blessing. She said something to Mama, that everything will end soon and things will be better. She said that Mama did the right thing by coming. . . .

From there we went to *Znamenskaya* church. On the way [we] saw the memorial for the 1,000 year anniversary of Russia, but it was too dark already, so we didn't get out. There were a lot of people in the streets, some crowding around the motors, in other words—everything as it should

46. Ioann Konstanovich, Andrei Vladimirovich [?].
47. St. Varvara the Martyr, an Orthodox saint.
48. Female elder or holy woman.

be. We went to the chapel where the Mother of God appeared in the oven and to 2 infirmaries. . . . There was a good amount of people at the station and trumpeters from Reserve regiments. They played the Ulan march and some waltz since we did not leave for a long time. They had to haul both motors into the train. Both bishops were there of course . . . they even climbed into the train and we hugged again. Your cavalry officer Nakashidze was there too. Remember him from Blagoveshensky hosp.[ital] with a serious head wound? I forgot to say that we also went to the orphanage for refugee boys, and they brought [more] from another one— the girls. On the train sat in little ones' car with Kolesnikov. Well, that's all.
May God keep you.
I kiss you affectionately, my Papa, my jewel.
Your *Plastun*.[49]

—

Wednesday. 30th December.
Mitya had a physical, later he came back and almost the entire time we sat together, played checkers and did just plain nothing. He is so good, Lord knows. . . . Grandma had breakfast. At 2 o'clock saw darling Papa off with Mama. So sad. From there to *Znamenie*. At 3 o'clock to a Christmas party at the House of Invalids. Later we 2 rode around in a troika with Isa. Had dinner with Mama in the playroom. In the evening talked with Mitya. Unexpectedly he received instructions to go to the Caucusus for about two days. So sad. Early to bed, have a head cold.

49. An infantry Cossack regiment.

1916

Russia continued to be a part of the war effort, but 1916 was no more successful than the previous year. Things were starting to look dire for the empire, and many of Nicholas's relatives believed that Rasputin's closeness to Alexandra and the children was casting a dark shadow over the Romanov dynasty. Much to her horror, Olga found out that her first cousin Dmitri, as well as her cousin-in-law, Felix Yusupov, were involved in the conspiracy and murder of Grigori Rasputin, in an effort to make the Romanovs appear once again stable in the eyes of many skeptical Russians. Olga documented her sadness over Rasputin's death, but seemed unaware of the poor shape that Russia's military was in, despite still being involved with local hospitals that treated the wounded.

—

From the memoirs of V. I. Chebotareva:
January 1916.
Tatiana Nikolaevna is so touchingly affectionate, was helping with preparations, sat in the corner [and] cleaned the instruments, and on the 4th came in the evening to boil the silk. . . . asked me about my childhood, if I had any brothers and sisters, where is my brother, what is his name. Finally [I] convinced her to go have [her] palm read. Rita arranged it in the prep room. [She] ran with curiosity. Olga assures [us] that she dreams of remaining a spinster, while Shakh-Bagov is reading on her palm that she will have twelve children. Tatiana Nikolaevna has an interesting palm: her life line suddenly stops and makes a sharp turn to the side. They assured us that this means she will pull off something unusual.

On the 6th, the heir came and was running in the hall in a wheelchair. Then he did not want to show the medals to Rita,[1] and started playing dominoes, got fascinated by glass fractions, spilled ink on himself, laid out the dominoes into indents and was very happy—[it looks like] "a sandwich with caviar."

16 January.
Today Tatiana Nikolaevna walked with me upstairs after [doing the] dressings, to do Popov's dressings. The poor child is terribly embarrassed; grabs my hand: "So awfully embarrassing and frightening . . . one never knows whom to acknowledge and whom not to." From Olga it sadly slipped out: "One cannot say anything on the telephone, [someone is always] listening in, they will report it, but not the truth, will lie like they did recently." What exactly she was referring to [I] did not have the chance to ask, but Voikov mentioned something—I never learned the details, evidently the "special censorship" is in its bloom.

. . . [I] was looking through some older memos. Seems [earlier] I missed Olga Nikolaevna's characteristic note "Dreams of happiness": "To get married, [to] always live in the countryside, winter and summer, [to] see only good people, no one official."

—

From a letter of a wounded officer, February 21, 1916:
I was a patient at the infirmary the entire April of 1916. The white nurses [nurses wearing white?] and kind doctors I thank very very much. . . .

1. Margarita Khitrovo ("Ritka") (1895–1952), lady-in-waiting and friend of Olga Nikolaevna.

"When the Tsar's children came to visit,
It became easier to breathe for all,
The suffering suddenly went away
From us ailing soldiers,
And even in our future anguish,
Perhaps already gray haired,
We will remember these visits,
Like magic childhood dreams . . ."
Your Imperial Majesty's Hussar, Posadnoy. 21/II/1916

—

From the memoirs of V. I. Chebotareva:
February 1916.

Tatiana Nikolaevna cross-examined what O. said—since [he] returned from Evpatoria. [She] was apparently waiting to hear about K.: "They went for six weeks, didn't they?" They say that K. is returning any day. And plus a letter came from Shakh-Bagov—Olga Nikolaevna threw all her things around from delight, and threw a pillow up on a top shelf. She felt feverish and she jumped around: "Can someone have a stroke at 20 years old? I think I am having a stroke!" But Varvara Afanasievna declared: "Young blood is warm; the years pass, and the blood cools off."

—

Wednesday. 30th March.
After [getting] a massage to the infirmary. Did the same things as always. Mama came after the service. During the day we 2 rode with her. At 4 o'clock to the Red Cross for *moleben*. Had a music lesson. Aunt Mavra and Elena had dinner, and after that she read to us a long letter from Vera, "about those awful days they lived through in Montenegrin and about [their] miraculous redemption . . ." and about

many more [things] that happened to them. Anya came over at 10 o'clock. At 11 o'clock to bed. Papa telegraphed, [he] departed from Kamenetz-Podolsk.

Wednesday. 6th April.
To church in the morning and in the evening. Aleksei has awful pains in his arm. He did not sleep all night. During the day [he was] lying down in the playroom. We sat with him and Mama and painted. Rode with Trina. In the evening 2 [degrees] and heavy fog. At 10 o'clock [we] confessed downstairs. Papa telegraphed.

Tuesday. 12th April.
Maria, Anastasia, Isa and I went to inspect my medical train #4. From there to the infirmary. Papa telegraphed from Smolensk. At 2 o'clock went to Matveyesky infirmary with Mama, after that to the Red Cross. Rode with Nastenka. Again after 6 o'clock. Dmitri had tea and at 3 1/2 we 5 with him and Mama to a concert at Anya's. . . . Mama is very tired.

—

From the memoirs of nurse S. Y. Ofrosimova:[2]
In my mind's eye I see them [the grand duchesses] again, sitting across from me as in that distant past.

Diagonally from me is the Grand Duchess Olga Nikolaevna. She draws me to her with irresistible force—the force of her charm. I almost cannot work when she is sitting that close to me, I just keep looking at her enchanting little face.

And only then, when my eyes meet her intelligent, kind and gentle eyes, do I look down at my own work, embarrassed and confused when she starts talking amiably to me. . . .

2. S. Y. Ofrosimova worked at the infirmary with the grand duchesses.

She cannot be called beautiful, but all of her being exudes such femininity and such youth, that she seems more than beautiful. The more you look at her, the more comely and more charming is her face. It is illuminated by an inner light, it appears more and more wondrous with each bright smile, her manner of laughing, throwing her head back, so that you can see the even row of her snow-white pearly teeth.

Skillfully and deftly, her unusually beautiful and delicate hands perform their work. In a particularly careful and loving manner, all of her fragile and delicate being leans over soldier's shirt which she is sewing. . . .

One cannot help but recall the words spoken to me by one of her tutors: "Olga Nikolaevna has a crystal soul."

—

Friday. 15th April.
Walked to the infirmary with the little ones.[3] . . . At 2 o'clock went to Kokorevsky infirmary with Mama, and after 3 o'clock met darling Papa. [We] broke the ice remnants with the sailors under the bridge. Papa and Mama took a walk. She—in a wheelchair. After tea, [we] rode with Isa. In the evening Papa read to us.

Tuesday. 26th April.
Massage and to the infirmary. Mama also. Papa arrived yesterday.[4] Ate with Mama, tea and dinner on the balcony. Warm, a little windy. . . . We 4 rode with Nastenka. Had a singing lesson. Helped Aleksei with homework, later rode with him and Vladimir Nikolaevich. In the evening went to our [infirmary] to clean the instruments. Mama has facial pains again and [her] heart [is] not too good.

3. "The little pair": Maria and Anastasia.
4. Again from Stavka, the military headquarters in Mogilev.

—

From the memoir of V. I. Chebotareva:
May 1916.

Olga Nikolaevna got seriously attached to Shakh Bagov, but it is so pure, naive and hopeless. Strange, unique girl. [She] does not give away her feelings for anything. It is only revealed by a special affectionate timbre in her voice, with which she gives [him] instructions: "Please hold the pillow higher. Are you not tired? Are you not bored?" When he left, the poor thing sat alone for an hour, with her nose in the sewing machine, and sewed so persistently, determinedly. Evidently she inherited her mother's personality. The empress said that she "fell in love with the emperor at twelve years old . . . but did everything for this marriage not to take place. There is no happiness on this earth, or else one pays dearly for it." And she paid, dearly, for her own. Is the same fate in store for Olga? She looked assiduously for the pencil-sharpening blade which Shakh Bagov used on the evening of his departure . . . looked for it all morning and was so happy when she found it. She also saved the calendar page from 6th June, the day of his departure.

—

Thursday. 19th May.
At 9 1/2 we 4 with Mama to our grotto church. Then to the infirmary. Today is the first anniversary of Mitya's being wounded. Iedigarov had dinner and later . . . told us a mass of interesting things about his trip to Persia. Papa and Aleksei wrote to Mama.[5]

5. Meaning Alexandra received letters from them.

Friday. 20th May.
At 10 o'clock to Znamenie with T. and to the infirmary. M. and A.⁶ gave us a lift. Mama came later. Around 12 o'clock Boris Ravtopulo and Mitya arrived. Both with completely shaved heads. Awfully nice to see them. Stood by the window. Trina had breakfast. During the day we 4 rode with her. Sunny, warmer. Had a long singing lesson. Took photos on the balcony of our infirmary. Papa wrote to Mama. Aleksei too. In the evening Mama sang a little.

Thursday. 26th May.
Ate with Mama on the balcony. After 2 o'cl. went to the Grand palace with her. After that rode around. Overcast. Rain after tea. Gathered forget-me-nots and lilies-of-the-valley with her on the Children's Island. After 10 o'cl. to bed. Papa wrote. The news is [good] thank God.

Saturday. 28th May.
Very warm, even hot. Tea on the balcony. Papa wrote. Went to *vsenoshnaya*. Everything is covered with birch trees, so cozy. Mama is tired. In the evening to the infirmary. Left after 12 o'clock.

Saturday. 4th June.
Viktor Erastovich was wounded, Skvotrsov too, but lightly, and 7 Cossacks. 1 was killed. Shurik is ill with typhus. To *Znamenie* and to the infirmary with Mama. Mitya and Borya came before 1 o'clock. Did all as usual. Raining and cold. Anya and Emma Fredericks with her father had breakfast again. During the day rode with Mama in 2 equipages. [We] were cold and wet. Saw Mitya from the Silayevs' window.

6. Maria and Anastasia.

Papa wrote. Went to *vsenoshnaya*. In the evening to the infirmary. After 9 o'cl. Mitya and Boris came over. Cleaned instruments and sewed pillows.

Friday. 10th June.
At 9 1/2 we 4 and Mama—to *obednya*. Uncovering of the relics of holy Ioann of Tobolsk.[7] During the day we worked in the warehouse of the Grand palace. Dmitri [Pavlovich] had tea. Mama was very tired. Papa wrote.

—

A. Popov, cornet {officer} of the 8th Hussar-Lubensky regiment, 12 June 1916:
I will remember always how I enjoyed my stay at the infirmary. The days when the Empress and the Grand Duchesses visited the infirmary—the brightest days of my life.

—

Thursday. 16th June.
Ate on the balcony. During the day there again, and warmed up in the sun. After tea, with Mama received 5 nurses who were going to Germany. And 4—to Austria. At 6 o'clock went to the garden. Picked flowers with the Derevenkoes.[8] The weather is wonderfully summery. Papa and Aleksei wrote.

Friday. 17th June.
At 12 1/2 went to the church graveyard for the colonel's funeral. Ate on the balcony. During the day rode with Isa. At 4 o'clock, cinematograph at the Manege, a French film. Hot, nice. Papa wrote.

7. Metropolitan of Tobolsk in early eighteenth century, later an Orthodox saint whose feast day is 10 June.
8. Dr. Vladimir Nikolaevich Derevenko, a court physician, and his son Kolya.

Wednesday. 22nd June.

Today is a year from the time when the Little One[9] left us for the first time. At 3 o'clock Mama, Anya and I went for a ride. The weather was wonderful. We gathered flowers in the field behind the woods. In the evening—to the infirmary. Mama—also.

———

From a letter of Second Lieutenant Vlanimirsky, Leib. Guard of Lithuanian Regiment, 1916:

It was such joy to see the Empress and the Grand Duchesses, a pleasure to hear their kind words addressed to us, simple soldiers—this memory will never leave our minds, not in good times, not in bad. A big, simple, Russian "Thank You" to the medical personnel for all their attention and care. I am leaving the Infirmary with sadness, a feeling that here I spent the best, the most peaceful and blissful minutes of my life.

———

Sunday. 26th June.

To *obednya* with Mama. Sandro had breakfast on the balcony. Really hot and nice. Not one cloud all day. Papa wrote. At 2 o'clock we 2 with Isa—to the city for the consecration of her hospital for 250 children of the refugees! It was long and boring. The building is excellent. Returned for tea. Later lay out in the sun. Mama went to the dentist. In the evening to the infirmary. Stayed until almost 1 o'clock. Everyone played croquet, [I] sewed pillowcases.

9. Aleksei had accompanied his father to the military headquarters in 1915.

Thursday. 30th June.
Papa did not write, has no time, but Aleksei did. In the evening to the infirmary without Mama. Got home after 11 o'clock. Mama has a headache.

Thursday. 14th July.
Mama and I received German and Austrian nurses. In the evening went to the infirmary. Mama—later. When the cornet arrived, we went into the sitting room. At first he played the fiddle, and I on the piano in the light of one lamp, then he sang in the dark, since it wasn't that scary.

Monday. 18th July.
There was some news about the battalion—16 killed and 76 wounded.

Wednesday. 20th July.
Stopped by Anya's to pick up Mama and to the infirmary. Wrote a lot, took flowers around and etc. Cold and sunny in the evening. Ate on the balcony. Papa wrote. At 2 hrs 20 min. we 2 with Isa—to the city for the charities and small committee.

Friday. 5th August.
At 10 o'clock to *Znamenie* with Mama and to the infirmary. We have 5 new [patients]. All heavily [wounded]. Zaremba had surgery in the evening due to bleeding. After that rode around with Mama and Anya in 2 carriages. In Pavlovsk, while we were picking flowers, Mama's horse on the right suddenly fell down. Returned all together. In the evening to the infirmary—we 4 without Mama. Shupp and Chizhik said goodbye to Mama. Leaving tomorrow. Very sad. Home at 11.45.

Formal portrait of the Russian imperial family prior to World War I. Left to right: Olga, Maria, Nicholas II, Alexandra, Anastasia, Aleksei, and Tatiana. (*Library of Congress*)

Olga reading on the beach in the Crimea, c. 1913. (*Yale University Library*)

Dowager Empress Maria Fedorovna ("grandma"), c. 1907. (*Yale University Library*)

Tsar Nicholas II and his son and heir Aleksei. (*Yale University Library*)

Nicholas II with his four daughters: Tatiana, Anastasia, Maria, and Olga, c. 1916. (*Yale University Library*)

Nicholas II and Aleksei reviewing naval troops in 1916. (*Yale University Library*)

In the imperial train c. 1916, back row, left to right: Grand Duke Dmitri, Nicholas II, Alexandra, Grand Duke Michael Alexandrovich ("Uncle Misha"), Tatiana, and Olga. Front: Anastasia and Maria. (*Yale University Library*)

Olga dancing with an officer on the deck of the *Polar Star*, her grandmother's imperial yacht, shortly before the war. (*Yale University Library*)

The grand duchesses kayaking with their father in one of the Alexander Park canals. Left to right: Olga, Tatiana, Maria, and Nicholas II. Anastasia may be taking this photo. (*Yale University Library*)

Olga with her friend Pavel Voronov, c. 1911. Voronov was Olga's strongest love interest. In 1914, shortly after Voronov got married, an obviously heartbroken Olga wrote in code in her diary: "T. was there with my S [Voronov]. (In the end he is S. to me, for the bride [has] the rest of him, but for me [he is] S." (*Yale University Library*)

Officer Rodionov, Tatiana, Anastasia, Nicholas II, and Olga on the tennis court, c. 1914. (*Yale University Library*)

Pierre Gilliard, the grand duchesses' tutor, with Olga and Tatiana, c. 1912. (*Yale University Library*)

Olga on a bicycle with Anastasia on foot in Alexander Park shortly before the revolution. (*Yale University Library*)

Olga and Anna Vyrubova in 1915. Vyrubova is in a wheelchair as a result of a serious train accident earlier that year. (*Yale University Library*)

Olga with Alexandra at the Alexander Palace, c. 1913. (*Yale University Library*)

"We 2" Olga and Tatiana. (*Yale University Library*)

Olga in her nurse uniform. (*Yale University Library*)

Nicholas II dressed in a Cossack uniform visiting Cossack troops at the front during World War I. (*Wire Service*)

Alexandra holds a camera while watching a photographer set up his equipment. In the background is the infirmary where Olga, her mother, and sister Tatiana worked. (*Yale University Library*)

Maria (left) and Anastasia posing with patients at their infirmary. (*Yale University Library*)

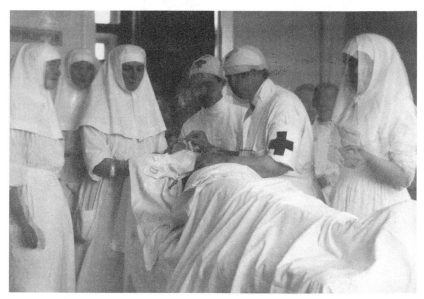

Assisting in surgery. Left to right, Olga, Tatiana, and Alexandra. Valentina Ivanovna Chebotareva is on the far right. (*Yale University Library*)

Olga (standing in the back row, right), Alexandra (next to Olga), and Tatiana (sitting) posing with patients at the infirmary. Dr. (Princess) Gedroitz is next to Alexandra, third from the left. (*Yale University Library*)

Olga, right, in her nurse uniform, taking notes. (*Yale University Library*)

The secret code Olga occasionally used in her diaries. (*GARF*)

ACCEPTS 15 AMBULANCES.

Czarina and Grand Duchess Grateful for American Gift.

PETROGRAD, Sept. 24, (via London.) —Fifteen motor ambulances of the field hospital presented by a group of Americans were formally accepted today by Czarina Alexandra and Grand Duchess Tatiana. The presentation was made by Captain Philip Lydig and Dr. Philip Newton.

The ambulances were lined up in front of the palace at Tsarskoe Selo, when the Empress and the Grand Duchesses Tatiana and Olga, dressed in the simple costume of hospital nurses, appeared and inspected them, expressing their appreciation and thanks many times. Following the ceremony the ambulances passed in review before the members of the imperial family and then returned to Petrograd.

The new cars will be known as "the American Ambulance of Her Imperial Highness Grand Duchess Tatiana Nicolaievna." They will be sent to the front tomorrow under command of Dr. Newton.

From the *New York Times*, September 24, 1915.

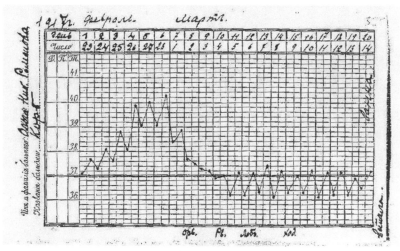

Temperature chart dated February/March 1917 for patient "Olga Nik. Romanova," inserted in her diary pages. (*GARF*)

The last page of Olga's diary, dated "March 15th. Wednesday [1917]." (*GARF*)

Tatiana (center) working in the Alexander Palace vegetable garden shortly after their arrest in March 1917 by the Provisional Government. Anastasia ("Nastenka") Hendrikova is helping Tatiana. Nicholas II is on the right of Tatiana holding a shovel. (*Yale University Library*)

Alexandra in her wheelchair in Alexander Park sometime after the family's arrest. (*Yale University Library*)

Olga, Aleksei, and Anastasia resting after working in the vegetable garden in Alexander Park, May 1917. (*Library of Congress*)

Alexander Kerensky, head of the Russian Provisional Government, about the time the imperial family was arrested. Kerensky was overthrown by Lenin and his Bolshevik Party on November 7, 1917. (*Wire Service*)

The imperial family and guards outside of the Governor's House, Tobolsk, Siberia. The family was interred at this house from late August 1917 to April 1918 when they were removed to Ekaterinburg in the Urals. (*Library of Congress*)

Nicholas II and his children sunning themselves on a barn roof in Tobolsk. They would all be murdered in Ekaterinburg on July 16, 1918. Sitting from left to right, Olga, Anastasia, Nicholas II, Aleksei, and Tatiana. Maria is standing. (*Wire Service*)

Thursday. 11th August.
Today is a year anniversary of the famous balcony. With Mama to Znamenie and the infirmary. Again [it's] cold and damp. Trina had breakfast on the balcony. During the day Funk[10] took our photographs. The day got clearer. Papa wrote. As of yesterday, our infirmary is referred to as "Mama's Personal." And we are part of the nursing team. In the evening at 8 o'clock to the infirmary—with Mama. Cleaned instruments. Tatiana boiled the silks. Bibi needed to have 100 huge towels cut up immediately. Which is what we all did until 1 o'clock in the morning. Count Reich had intestinal blockage, and they brought him to us. He may need a laparotomy. Everyone played "ruble."

Friday. 12th August.
With Mama to *Znamenie* and to the infirmary. [I was] lying down in the hammock and read the second part of "Surgery." Warmer than yesterday. Papa wrote. Tea on the balcony. Rode bicycles with Maria, Anastasia and the Derevenko children.

Tuesday. 16th August.
Yesterday Romania declared war on Austria. What fools, they could have done this earlier. But then today, Germany declared war on them. To *Znamenie* and to the infirmary. Ran around. Ate at home. The weather is nasty. Took photos with the wounded in the Grand Palace with Mama.

Friday. 19th August.
The weather is overcast, fresh. Sat upstairs at home. T. and Mama went to the Red Cross. Papa wrote. Count Fredericks

10. Presumably the photographer.

had tea. Maria and I are reading "The Wide Wide World."
In the evening to the infirmary with Mama. Rained.

Friday. 9th September.
With Mama to Znamenie and to the infirmary. At 10 1/2 she
went to the city to visit the dying countess Hendrikova.[11] [I]
went to the infirmary with M. and A. There were 4 of our
wounded Cossacks. . . . They told us a lot, the darlings. Later,
rode around with Isa and T. Anya had tea. Papa wrote. Sunny
all day. The leaves are falling.

Saturday. 10th September.
Countess Hendrikova died during the night. Went to
Znamenie with Mama and to the infirmary. Ate with Mama
and Anya. At 2 1/2 looked at the medical motor named after
Tatiana from the Americans. At 3 o'cl. went with Mama to
the Hussar's barracks where 52 children of the reserves reside.
They were doing gymnastics and singing. Going to *vsenoshnaya* without Mama. She is tired and doesn't feel well. Papa
wrote. We 3 went with Mama to the *panikhida* for Countess
Hendrikova. The entire family was there. Returned after 10
o'clock.

Sunday. 11th September.
We 4 in the Grotto church for *obednya*. After that—to the
infirmary. Mama—later. Boris was there. Rainy, overcast. Ate
with Mama. At 2 o'clock, Kasyanov said farewells. Keep him
safe, Lord. We 4 went to the Grand Palace. Sat at home. Had
my hair washed.

Monday. 12th September.
In the morning to the infirmary. Mama later, since she was

11. Nastenka Hendrikova's mother.

tired. . . all [was] as usual, a lot of running around, but I love it, makes me feel like I am accomplishing something. Ate with Mama. At 3 o'cl. rode with M., Mama and Anya in 2 carriages. T. and Shvybz[12]—astride [on horses]. Sunny and rather warm. Papa wrote. Anya had tea. [I] long to see Mitya.

Tuesday. 20th September.
Directly to the infirmary. Maria Pavlovna (the younger)[13] had breakfast and rode with us 4 during the day. After tea we 3 with Trina went to see Aunt Olga's medical train #87. Many wounded guards. Papa wrote. Mama is receiving again. We got 3 more wounded [patients]. [I] sat with them for a long time and darned stockings.

Wednesday. 28th September.
Mama stayed in bed all day, but received Sturmer[14] at 6 o'clock. Around 3 o'cl. We 2 took a ride on the motor and went to the Silayevs'. Sat upstairs with Mitya's mama and [I] was so happy, at least it felt like a part of him. Later had tea with them and ate various pastries brought over from the Caucasus. In the evening—to the infirmary. Bibi got a telegram from Mitya.

Thursday. 29th September.
Sonia Dehn had tea. Papa wrote. Went to the Grand Palace with M. and A. After that we 4 took a ride in the motor. Did some trying on [of clothes?]. In the evening—to the infirmary. L.'s Symphony orchestra from the Volynsky regiment. They played excellently. I stood in the doors: went to see all

12. Anastasia.
13. Maria Pavlovna (1890–1958), daughter of Pavel Alexandrovich, sister of Dmitri Pavlovich, and Nicholas's first cousin.
14. Boris Sturmer (1848–1917), served as prime minister, foreign minister, and interior minister of the Russian empire for several months during 1916

the other and saw the little Montenegrin. He is so eternally charming. Saw Mitya's mama from the window.

Sunday. 2nd October.
[We] had our hair curled, went to *obednya* in the grotto church, after that—to the infirmary. Trina and Nastenka had breakfast. At 3 o'cl. stopped by *Znamenie* with Mama and [then] boarded the train. Rain, snow, nasty. Met Mitya's mama. Going with us are Shvedov, Anya, Isa, Botkin, Resin, and Kern. Papa wrote.

Saturday. 15th October.
With Mama to *Znamenie* and the infirmary. Freezing, overcast. Trina had breakfast. We 4 went to the Grand Palace, later took a ride on the motor. Rode by Mitya's mama's [house] but she wasn't home, we did see her yesterday morning and today. Papa wrote. Anya had tea. Going to *vsenoshnaya* with Mama. We 4 went to the infirmary. Was talking in the front room with Kulnev when suddenly Mitya walked in. So awfully happy to see him with a part in his hair. Stood in the hallway and sat. [I] darned socks.

Saturday. 22nd October.
With Mama to *Znamenie* and the infirmary. Took photos again because they didn't come out last time. During the day took a walk like yesterday. Rather warm. No snow, 5 [deg.] Aleksei has the 2 Makarovs, Zhenya and Lelya visiting since yesterday. Everyone was at *vsenoshnaya*. Did nothing unusual in the evening.

Sunday. 23rd October.
We 2 to the early service at the grotto church, then—to the infirmary. Saw Mitya from the window. Left at 12 o'cl.

Tzvetinsky and Dmitri had breakfast. During the day took a walk with Papa and Mama. After tea [had] a small cinematograph in Aleksei's [room]. They are leaving today. Ate all together. After 10 o'cl. came over and read Sladkopevtsev's funny short stories. At 11 1/2 to bed.

Friday. 28th October.
We 4 with Mama had breakfast on the train on the way to the city. T. and I went to her committee, after which I received O. B. Stolypina.[15] The Little Ones[16] went around the infirmary at the Grand Palace with Mama. There are currently 358 people there. Tea on the train with Viktor Erastovich. It's drizzling and awfully dark, but warm. Now Mama is receiving. Papa telegraphed from Kiev. They went to Grandma's for her fiftieth wedding anniversary.[17] In the evening we 4—to the infirmary. Played the piano in the sitting room. Mitya came in toward the end. Returned after 11 o'clock. Rain.

Monday. 31st October.
Mitya and [his] mama evidently went to the Caucasus, since the shutters [of their house] were closed. To *Znamenie* and to the infirmary with Mama. Dzhurkovich fussed all morning, got dressed and at 12 o'cl. went with Daragan to Yalta to [see] Popov. So sad, we got so used to him after all, and despite everything he is a very good person. Rode around Pavlovsk with Mama in a carriage. Cold, dark and rainy. Later we 4— in a motor in Pavlovsk. Mama is receiving the whole time. Papa and Aleksei wrote to her. In the evening to the infir-

15. Widow of the Prime Minister Pyotr Arkadievich, who was assassinated at a theater in Kiev in 1911 in front of Tsar Nicholas and Olga and Tatiana.
16. Again, Maria and Anastasia.
17. The dowager empress was living in Kiev at the time.

mary with Mama. Little Dzhurkovich is missed so much, in the rooms and in everything. He was always taking walks up and down the hallway or in the sitting room, etc. Returned in an open motor. Snowing a little.

Thursday. 3rd November.[18]
21 years old. To *Znamenie* and to the infirmary with Mama. Not much to do. At 12 o'clock *moleben*, and home at 1 1/2. Sunny, cold. Papa and Aleksei wrote to me, such dears. Received a lot of telegrams and letters. From our [friends and relatives] in Yalta, etc. Dmitri had tea. Responded to letters and telegrams the entire time. In the evening to the infirmary with Mama. Played the countess's piano in the ladies room. Mitya sent Bibi a telegram from Mozdok. Left after 11 1/4.

Tuesday. 8th November.
To *Znamenie* and the infirmary with Mama. To everyone's joy Kasyanov arrived. He lay in his old spot with a wounded right hip by an exploded bullet. Lost weight, head is shaved, but still charming. During the day we 4 rode around with Mama. Had a singing lesson, and now—music.

Wednesday. 30th November.
T. played the countess's piano in the ladies' room for Kasyanov. Heard absolutely nothing from Mitya. Ate together. At 2 o'clock Mama and I received a Norwegian young lady. After that, took a walk with Papa. It's snowing a little and [there is] snow on the ground. Aunt Ella came over, had tea. Sat with her until 7 o'cl. while Mama received Uncle Mekko[?]. They had some serious discussions. Holy God help us. She [Aunt Ella] also had dinner. Went to Al.[eksei's]

18. Olga's birthday.

to say goodbye. Papa and M. pasted [photos] into the album. After 11 o'cl. to bed. Read *V gostyakh u turok* [Visiting the Turks] by Leikin.

Saturday. 3rd December.
To *Znamenie* and to the infirmary. Mama and Aleksei came at 11 o'clock for Colonel Dzerzhinsky's surgery. Excised (with Novocain) some fatty tumors from his shoulders. Al. stood in the door the entire time. Later he played "ruble" with everyone. Ate all together. During the day at 2 3/4 took a walk with Papa and Mama like yesterday. Very dark and slippery. Will all go to *vsenoshnaya*. In the evening Papa pasted [photos into] the album, Tatiana read "Gdye apelsini zreyut" [Where the Oranges Blossom].

Tuesday. 6th December.
At 10? to *obednya* with Mama. [Received] congratulations in the small room. After 2 o'cl. Took a ride like yesterday. It's snowing, warmer. During tea received a telegram from Papa, who writes, "Today, you are appointed the Chief of the Second Kubansky battalion. I congratulate you on this appointment and hug all of you. Papa." I am so joyful and happy and proud, can't even describe it. Had dinner early, and to the infirmary with Mama. Played the piano. Left at 11 1/2 . 6 hr 25 min.

Sunday. 11th December.
On the train between Novgorod and M[illegible] across the r[iver] Kerest. Departed tonight at 3:10 and arrived in Novgorod at 9 1/2 in the morning. At 10 went to *Sofiysky* Cathedral. There was an *Arkhireisky* service and *moleben* until 12, paid respects to various holy relics. Downstairs stopped by the storeroom with ancient artifacts and got home by 1:00

o'clock. At 2 o'clock, went to Zemskaya Hospital, and my female mon.[astery—i.e. nunnery] . . . kissed the icons, etc. . . . then to the orphanage of the refugee children, and Yurevsky male monast.[ery], [located] 5 *versts*[19] from the city. Drank tea at the table with the nobles. From there to the chapel, where Our Lord's Mother appeared in sorrow, and remained. Terribly nice and such a wonderful smell in the chapel. Was able to fall asleep before Tsarskoe, where we arrived at 12 hrs 20 min. at night.

Saturday. 17th December.
We 2 to *Znamenie*. Did everything as usual, made up the beds, etc. Sokolov is gloomier than dark night. Played *bloshki* [tiddlywinks] with Kasyanov against T.[atiana] and Ulan.[20] Ate with Mama. Anya drank tea, had dinner. Sat all day with Mama. Father Grigori[21] is missing since last night. They are looking for him everywhere—awfully hard. Attended *vsenoshnaya* here at the house. In the evening, Mama, Anya, confessed. Lili Dehn[22] was here. Papa wrote. Sat almost until 12 o'clock. Everyone was waiting for a telephone [call] from Kalinin, etc.[23] Slept all 4 together. Lord help us.

Monday. 19th December.
As usual, to *Znamenie* and to the infirmary. Almost nothing to do. Went with Kasyanov to the drawing room and behind closed doors, without anyone present, I played and he sang various new beautiful things. Ate with Mama. Found out for certain that Father Grigori was murdered, most likely by Dmitri[24] and thrown from a bridge by Khrestovky. They

19. Approximately three and a half miles.
20. From the Ulansky regiment.
21. Rasputin was killed the previous evening.
22. Alexandra's lady-in-waiting and companion.
23. Presumably for news about Rasputin
24. He was presumed to be just one of the conspirators involved in the murder.

found him in the water. It's so terrible, should not even write. Sat and drank tea with Lillie and Anya and the entire time felt Father Gregori with us . . . at 6 o'clock met Papa and Aleksei. Such joy. Had dinner together. After 10 o'clock Papa and Mama received Kalinin, then Uncle Pavel. We were in Anya's rooms. At 12 o'clock to bed.

Saturday. 24th December.
During the day took a walk with Papa. Lots of snow. Bright night, in the evening 12 [degrees] of frost. At 3 o'cl., a Christmas party in the hallway. After that went with Mama to Anya's with a tree, and then we 4 [went] to [see] Nastenka, Isa, and Trina. At 4 1/2 our Christmas party in the playroom. At 6 1/2 with Papa to *vsenoshnaya*. Mama and Al. at 7 o'clock. In the evening stopped by [to see] Al. and just sat [with him]. Lord, save and have mercy on us. A very lovely *vsenoshnaya*. Got a ring from Zenaide,[25] a baby doll, a pillow, etc.

Christmas Day.
At 10 1/2 with Papa to *obednya*. Mama and Al. later. Ate all together. Beautiful bright sun, sky, 7 [degrees] of frost. At 2 everyone went to the arena for the Convoy's Christmas party. All dear ones were there. Looking at them is so soothing. Went for a walk with Papa for a half an hour—after that he and Mama received Kalinin. At 6 we 2 with Mama to our infirmary, a Christmas tree was set up in the drawing room. Everyone except Sokolov was gathered there—Mama gave out gifts to all. Left at 7. Mama received Prince Golytzin. After dinner [I] played, at Papa's request, religious things [music] and everyone went to Anya's where Father Grigori's entire family was present: Paraskovia, Feod[orovna], Mitya,[26]

25. Presumably Zinaida Yusopova, Felix's mother.
26. Rasputin's son Dmitri.

Matryona, and Varya.[27] They are leaving for Pokrovskoye[28] on Tuesday. Went to [see] Al.[eksei] and Zhenya.[29] At 11 to bed. Mama doesn't feel too well, but she is so brave. Save her, Lord.

—

From the memoirs of V. I. Chebotareva:
December 1916.
We suffered such anxieties during that 17th! I came by the infirmary around seven o'clock, the nurse on duty rushed over: "They reported on the telephone: Grigori was killed". . . . The children called: "We cannot come in the evening, we have a duty, must stay with mama." At eleven in the evening Elizaveta Nikolaevna called, the commandant told her husband—Yusupov killed [Rasputin], the body has not been found. Interesting, they already knew about this incident at two o'clock?

In the evening, they say, around five o'clock, [they] found out about the loss, tears, despair. On Sunday, she [Olga?] and Tatiana Nikolaevna went to confession. On Sunday, the children did not come at all, came on Monday, faces swollen from tears, looking at everyone suspiciously. In the middle of dressings, Tatiana went out, spoke to Varvara Afanasievna, started crying, returned to operating room, keeping from [crying] with difficulty. . . . Truly, today is a confirmation of Olga's remark: "Mama does not feel well, and is tired, sitting with papers all day, much to do, in the morning the entire bed is covered [with papers]."

27. Rasputin's daughters, Maria and Varvara.
28. Rasputin's hometown in Siberia near Tobolsk.
29. Aleksei's companion/playmate.

—

Saturday. 31st December.

We 2 to *Znamenie* and to the infirmary. Rita was helping to replace Val.[lentina] Iv.[anovna][30] in the operating room, and I was [helping] a little on the ward. Distributed medicines, etc. Wrote. In general not much to do, only during the dressing changes. Around 3 went home to get dressed and go to a party at the School for Nannies, but I and Papa walked a little more. Mama and Anya were at Al.'s He feels better, but doesn't get up yet. At 6 1/2 we 4 with Papa went to *vsenoshnaya*. Will stop by [to see] Al. to say good night. In the evening [we] will gather for prayers. Read [our] fortunes with Anya using wax and paper. Lord, save us and have mercy on us in 1917, the new year.

30. Valentina Ivanovna Chebotareva.

1917

In 1917, as in the previous war years, Russia was still deeply and disastrously involved in World War I. This year, however, would mark an incredible change for Olga and her family. Due to his poor leadership, her father was forced to abdicate his throne, ending over three hundred years of Romanov rule. Europe's last absolute autocrat finally fell and Olga was, at least in theory, no longer a Grand Duchess but a Russian citizen. At the same time, she, along with her siblings, came down with the measles and all were forced to shave their heads. The timing of the illness caused her family to remain in Tsarskoe Selo, which led to them getting arrested by the revolutionaries—which sealed their fate. In mid-March, Olga penned her final diary entry. There is no explanation to the abrupt ending of many years of recording her daily events and thoughts. Why she stopped on that particular day will perhaps remain a mystery, but it does coincide with the forced abdication of her father on March 15.

———

Year 1917

Sunday. 1st January.
At 10 1/2 we 4 with Papa to *obednya*. Al.[eksei] is getting better, took a walk with us and had breakfast. Mama as usual, [was] on the couch. Around 2 we 3 went to take a walk with Papa. At 3 o'clock we 2 rode to the infirmary. Stayed there until almost 7 o'clock. We have 12 new [patients], including critical. In the evening Papa read Chekhov to us, a short story *"Knyaginya"* ["The Duchess"]. At 11 to bed. Help us, Holy Father in the New Year.

Thursday. 5th January.
We 2 at the infirmary until 11 1/2. Volga is ill. Sister [nurse]
Shevchuk substituted for her, and I assisted. Made up the
beds and changed dressings of the wounded, etc., wrote.
After that, to church, the sisters and Papa were already there.
Mama [came] later. She doesn't feel well. Ate all together. Sat
at home, then at Mama's. Anya dictated and I wrote down
Father Grigori's letters. Did not go to *vsenoshnaya*. After din-
ner, until 9 1/2, after Papa went to say goodnight to Al. he
played various church music on the piano, same as yesterday.
In the evening [he] finished [reading] the short story
"Guseva" [to us]. Anya came over. To bed at 11 o'clock.

Saturday. 7th January.
We 2 rode around with Nastenka, 5 deg. of frost. In the
morning the sun is bright and [there is a] rainbow. Fredericks
had tea. All conversation is difficult. Sat at Anya's with Lili.
She lay down, high T°. Didn't go to *vsenoshnaya*. Mama feels
dreadful. She is so tired. Lord save her. Later Al. went to
Anya's with Mama. She feels just dreadful.[1]

Monday. 9th January.
To *Znamenie* and we 2 to the infirmary. Volga wasn't there and
the two of us, Rita and I, substituted. Made up the beds, distributed medicines, changed dressings for the wounded, etc.
During the day we 4 rode in the troika[2] with Isa. 3 deg. [of]
frost. In the morning lots of snow. Mama was lying on the
balcony. [We] were preparing for the Romanian ceremony
and that made me angry. The ceremony was successful, [I] sat
between Papa and Uncle Mimi. Mama was tired of course,
but looked very beautiful in a black and white scarf with a

1. Alexandra took the news of Rasputin's death very hard.
2. Three-horse sleigh.

diamond strip in her hair. At 10 o'clock everything was over. Papa read to us, Chekhov's "Ved'ma" [The Witch] and "V Sud" [To the Court of Law].

Tuesday. 10th January.
We 2 with Mama went to visit the grave of Father Grigori.[3] Today is his name day. Had a music lesson with T. In the evening Papa read to us, Chekhov's "Sobytie" [The Incident] and started "Vragi" [The Enemy].

Sunday. 15th January.
During the day 4 deg. frost. We 4 with Papa to *obednya*. After dinner went to Anya's where [we] sat in the drawing room by the fireplace, etc.

Tuesday. 17th January.
We 2 to *Znamenie* and to the infirmary. Kamenetsky's appendicitis surgery lasted for a long time. Karol of Rumania had breakfast with us and during the day [we] walked with him and Papa. Uncle Mimi[4] had dinner. Left at 10 o'clock. Later, until 11 hrs 25 min. Papa read to us "Shvedskaya spichka" [The Swedish Match] and "Kleveta" [Slander].

Sunday. 22nd January.
All with Papa to *obednya*. Mama and I a little later. During the day sat with Mama at Al.'s, he is not bad, but not allowed to get up, in case the streptococcus attacks the joints. After tea went to Al.'s, again, cinematograph. 25 of frost. Sunny and awfully cold. At 6 o'clock the Cossacks came over to Anya's:

3. Rasputin was originally buried in Alexander Park, not far from the palace. After the revolution his body was exhumed by the soldiers and burned. It is unknown where his charred remains ended up.
4. Grand Duke Mikhail Alexandrovich (1878–1918), youngest brother of Nicholas II.

AKonst,[5] Viktor, Yuzik and [his] brother. All sat by the fireplace, and roasted [ourselves]. One lamp was lit as always on the floor. Again there was a quarrel between me and AleksKonst. with Vikt.Gr.[6] over a chair. It was so merry with them, as always, and cozy. Had dinner all together. In the evening all at Anya's.

Wednesday. 25th January.
Today is the 40th day of Father Grigori's [death].[7] Unable to walk with Papa because [I] went to the Grand Palace. Later sat in Al.'s [room]. There was a cinematograph. Mama received [visitors] almost until 4 1/2. In the evening looked at photographs from the 4th of Oct [illegible].

Friday. 3rd February.
We 2 to the infirmary. Mama came later, also changed dressings and visited everyone. About 4 o'clock went to walk with Papa. It's snowing, cold. 12 [degrees] of frost. At 5 o'clock, we 4 [went] to Anya's infirmary for a concert. (Her name day), Makarov, De Lozari, Ramin and Gulesko's orchestra. Wonderful, fine and beautiful. Returned around 7 o'clock. Mama went to the grave of Father Grigori. [I] went to Al.'s, put together a puzzle, etc. In Mama's [rooms] saw Anya's parents, and [her] brother with Tina Tina. Tomorrow, Sunday [sic] is their wedding. After 11 o'clock to bed. Cold. Mama feels so-so.

———

From the diary of Nicholas II:
7th February. Tuesday.
Riots began in Petrograd a few days ago; unfortunately the military started to participate in them. What an awful feeling

5. Abbreviation for Alexander Konstantinovich.
6. Abbreviation for Viktor Grigorevich.
7. The fortieth-day anniversary of death is important in the Orthodox church.

to be so far away and receive only snippets of bad news! Stayed to [hear] the report for a while. During the day took a walk on the highway to Orsha. The weather was sunny. After dinner decided to leave for T.[sarskoe] S.[elo] as soon as possible and moved into the train at one in the morning.

—

Thursday. 9th February.
Today Mitya is 24 years old. Lord save him. We 2 to the infirm.[ary]. Did the same as always. Uncle Georgiy had breakfast, while Mama was in bed because of her heart, but got up later and sat with Al.[eksei]. [I] sat at home nursing a cold. [It is] warmer. Father Grigori's daughters visited Anya. In the evening Lili [Dehn] sat with us until 11 o'clock. [I] have a headache.

Friday. 10 February.
[I] have an earache—lying down—Polyakov[8] examined [me], and said it was the inflammation of the middle ear. Had breakfast with Papa and Linevich. Mama in daybed. During the day [I stayed] in bed. 36,8, 37,2, 38,2, 38,0.[9] At 6 lay down on the sofa in the Red Room . . . Mama and Papa came by. Fell asleep early until 12 o'clock, then almost didn't sleep at all.

The Great Fast. Monday. 13th February.
Slept terribly, had earache—[had] a warm compress, and Polyakov does not allow me [to go] to the Red Room, so I am in the bedroom on the couch. Papa stopped by before breakfast and after. Mama sat during the day. Anya too. Al. had breakfast with me. Trina had tea. Nastenka stopped by.

8. One of the imperial physicians.
9. Olga records her body temperature throughout the day (in Celsius).

In the evening Papa and Mama stopped by. T° 37,5 – 37,5 – 37,3 – 37,2. Fell asleep rather early.

Thursday. 16th February.
Slept well. Polyakov came by. T° 36,7 – 36,9 – 36,9—did not see Al.[eksei] His arm hurts and he is lying down, poor little one. I am sitting in the Red Room with M. She has a cough. . . . Mama stopped by in the morning. Sat here during the day—Papa was here, Anya was here. Nastenka had tea. I am reading "War and Peace" to M.[aria] – 37,1.

Sunday. 19 February.
In general slept well. T° 36,5 – 37,1 1/2—37,0. Shvybz[10] and M. were with me. They are also coughing. Polyakov was here. [I] lay in the Red Room. Mama and Papa sat and put together a small puzzle. Then Papa went for a walk. Anya and Syroboyarsky came by. Rimma and Katya Zborovskaya had tea with us 4. Then cinematograph downstairs. In the evening Mama, Papa, Anya and Lili were here. Wrote.

Wednesday. 22nd February.
    Before breakfast [I] stayed in bed. Papa came by. [I] ate with Al. in the Red Room. He has [temperature] over 37,0. At 2 o'clock Papa came to say goodbye and left. Awfully sad. Keep him and save him, dear Lord. Mama came by in the morning and sat during the day. Went with her to the playroom to Al. and had tea. It was nice and sunny there. Fedosya Stepan.[ovna] brought over Anya's milkmaid's two-week-old baby girl. T° 36,4 – 37,0 – 37,1 1/2 .

—

10. Anastasia.

From the memoirs of Anna Vyrubova (February 1917):

On that day, I did not feel well. After seeing the Emperor out, I lay down and wrote to the empress that I cannot come to tea. In the evening, Tatiana Nikolaevna came over with the news that Aleksei Nikolaevich and Olga Nikolaevna have measles. They caught it from the young cadet who came over to play with the heir ten days ago. The empress and I sat with the children for a long time that day because Olga Nikolaevna had an ear infection. The cadet was coughing suspiciously and the next day came down with measles. . . . I did not believe in the chance of contagion for myself. Despite high fever, the next day, 22 February, I forced myself to get up for dinner, when my friend Lilli Dehn came over. In the evening, the empress came to visit with the girls, but I was really dizzy and could hardly speak. . . . [Later] Maria and Anastasia started coughing suspiciously. . . . In the evening the empress sat by my bedside. Quietly, wrapped in a white shawl she came out with Maria Nikolaevna to the regiments, who were getting ready to leave the palace. Perhaps they would have left that night if not for the Empress and her brave daughter, who calmly went around to see the soldiers, encouraging them with words and affection, forgetting about the mortal danger they put themselves in.

For three days we did not know where the emperor was. Finally, a telegram arrived where he asked for Her Majesty and the children to come to him. At the same time came a "command" on the telephone from Rodzyanko[11] for Her Majesty to leave the palace with the children. The Empress responded that she cannot go anywhere since this would mean death to the children; to which Rodzyanko responded "when the house is burning—you bring all out!" The

11. Pavel Pavlovich Rodzyanko, a member of the Duma.

Empress came in the evening to talk to me about potential departure, she conferred with doctor Botkin how to bring me to the train, the doctors were against going. Nevertheless we prepared to leave, but the departure did not happen.

—

From the diary of Nicholas II:
1st March. Wednesday.
During the night [we] turned back from M. Vishra because Luban and Tosno turned out to be occupied by the rioters.[12] Rode to Valdai, Dno and Pskov, where stayed for the night. Saw Ruzky. He, Danilov and Savvich had dinner. Gatchina and Luga also turned out to be occupied. Shame and disgrace! Was not able to get to Tsarskoe Selo. But thoughts and feelings are constantly there! Poor Alix, how much she must suffer over these events! Lord help us!

2nd March. Thursday.
Ruzky came in the morning and read his very long telephone conversation with Rodzyanko. According to him, the situation in Petrograd is such that the Duma ministers are helpless to do anything since the soc.[ial]-dem[ocrat] party, in the form of the worker's committee, is struggling against them.

4th March. Saturday.
Slept well. At 10 o'cl. the good Alek came over. Then [I] went to [hear] reports. At 12 o'cl. [I] went to the platform to meet dear Mama, who arrived from Kiev. Took her to my [quarters] and had breakfast with her and our [people]. Sat for a long time and talked. Today, finally, received two telegrams from dear Alix. Took a walk. The weather was awful—cold and

12. At this time Nicholas II was attempting to return to Tsarskoe Selo from headquarters.

stormy. After tea received Alekseyev and Fredericks.[13] At 8 o'cl. went to dinner at Mama's and sat with her until 11 o'cl.

5th March. Sunday.
The wind was very strong during the night. The day was clear and cold. At 10 o'cl. went to *obednya*, Mama came later. She had breakfast and stayed with me until 3 o'cl. Took a walk in the little garden. After tea received N. I. Ivanov who returned from an assignment trip. He was at Tsarskoe Selo and saw Alix. Said goodbye to poor Count Fredericks and Voikov, whose presence here annoys everyone for some reason; they went to his estate in Pensen. county. At 8 o'cl. went to dinner at Mama's.

6th March. Monday.
Was very happy in the morning to receive two letters from dear Alix and two letters from Maria. The wife of Captain Golovkin of the Finland regiment brought them. Took a walk in the garden. Mama came for breakfast. We sat together until 3 o'cl. Took a walk; a snowstorm started again. After tea received Williams. At 8 o'cl. went to Mama's train.

———

From the memoirs of V. I. Chebotareva:
March 1917.

So many impressions that I did not have the energy to pick up the pen yesterday. I found out about the abdication only on the morning of the 4th, in Petrograd they pasted [notices] up on the evening of the 3rd. I will never forget that moment. It was snowing hard, cold, [I] ran into a worker who had the "News" flyer in his hands. Asked him to read it.

13. Count Vladimir Borisovich Fredericks (1838–1927), minister of the Imperial Court.

[There was] a big crowd around [me] so I was forced to read these fatal words not in privacy; he abdicated for himself and for his son. Five days and the monarchy was gone. A stroke of a pen—and the century-old system collapsed. Silence all around. Everyone feels the horror. Russia—and without a Tsar.

At the infirmary, deathly silence. All are shocked, shaken. Princess Gedroitz [Vera Ignatievna] sobbed like a helpless child. We were expecting a constitutional monarchy and suddenly the throne was passed over to the people, and in [our] future—[was] a republic . . .

—

From the diary of Nicholas II:
8th March. Wednesday.
Last day in Mogilev. At 10 o'cl. signed the farewell command for the armies. At 1 1/2 o'cl. went to the guard house where [I] said goodbye to all the headquarters ranks and commands. At home said goodbye to the officers and convoy and regiment Cossacks—my heart almost broke! At 12 o'cl. went to mama's train car, had breakfast with her and her suite, and sat with her until 4 1/2 o'cl. Said goodbye to her, Sandro, Sergei, Boris and Alek. Poor Nilov was not allowed to go with me. At 4.45 departed Mogilev, a group of people saw me off touchingly. 4 members of the Duma escorted me to my train! Headed to Orsha and Vitebsk. The weather is frosty and windy. Grueling, painful and dreary.

9th March. Thursday.
Arrived in Tsarskoe Selo quickly and safely—at 11 o'cl. But Lord, what a difference, on the streets and around the palace, in the park are guards, and inside, in the hall some kind of ensigns! Went upstairs and there saw darling Alix and the

dear children. She looked healthy and vigorous, and they all were in beds in a dark room. But everyone feels well, except Maria who just caught measles recently. Had breakfast and dinner in Aleksei's playroom. Saw the good Benkendorf. Took a walk with Valya Dolg.[oruky] and worked with him in the garden for a bit, since we were not allowed to go any farther! After tea unpacked some clothes. In the evening went to see all the residents on the other side [of the palace], they were there altogether.

—

From the memoirs of Anna Vyrubova:

I had never seen and most likely will never see such an emotional strength that Her Majesty and her children had. "You know, Anya, with the Emperor's abdication all is finished for Russia," the Empress said, "but we should blame neither the Russian people nor the soldiers: it is not their fault."

Olga, and Tatiana and Aleksei Nikolaevich started to get better, when the last one—Maria Nikolaevna, got sick.

—

From the diary of Nicholas II:
10th March. Friday.
Slept well. Despite the situation in which we now find ourselves, the thought of being all together makes one feel happy and reassured. In the morning received Benkendorf, and then reviewed, organized and burned papers. Sat with the children until 2 1/2 o'cl. Took a walk with Valya Dolg.[oruky] [along] with the escort of the same two ensigns—today they were somewhat more polite. Had a nice workout [shoveling] snow. The weather was sunny. Spent the evening together.

11th March. Saturday.
Received Benkendorf in the morning, found out from him that we will be staying here for a rather long time. This is a pleasant awareness. Continued to burn letters and papers. Anastasia got an earache—the same as with the others. From 3 o'cl. until 4 1/2 o'cl. walked in the garden with Valya D. and worked in the garden. The weather was unpleasant, windy, 2° of frost. At 6.45 went to the *vsenoshnaya* at the campaign church. Aleksei took his first bath. Stopped by Anya's and Lilly D.[ehn]'s and then [went to see] all the rest.

12th March. Sunday.
It started to get warmer. In the morning Benkendorf and Apraksin were here; the latter is leaving Alix and said good-bye to us. At 11 o'cl. went to *obednya*. Aleksei got up today. Olga and Tatiana feel a lot better, while Maria and Anastasia are worse, headaches and earaches and vomiting. Took a walk and worked in the garden with Valya D. After tea, continued to put papers in order. In the evening made rounds of the house residents.

13th March. Monday.
Keeps getting warmer, the day was semi-overcast. Took a walk in the morning for a half hour. Kept busy with old business. Maria keeps having high temperature [of] 40.6, and Anastasia has earache. The rest felt well. Took a walk during the day and worked. In the evening sat at Anya's with Lilly D.

14th March.
A gray and warm day. Took a walk with Valya D. in the morning for three quarters of an hour. Right now—[there is] a lot of time to read for pleasure, although I spend a lot of time sitting upstairs with the children. Maria keeps having

high temperature—40.6. Anastasia is having complications with her ears, even though yesterday they drained her right ear. During the day took a walk around the entire park.

15th March. Wednesday.
Lovely sunny frosty day. Took a nice walk with Valya D., and as is usual now, escorted by one of the guards. Maria and Anastasia's condition is the same as yesterday; slept badly and Maria's fever [was] the highest to date, as during the day it was 40.9. The rest have completely recovered. Walked and worked a lot during the day. Read before dinner, and sat with the children in the evening until 10 o'cl., and the two of us had tea.

—

Olga Romanov's final diary entry:
15th March. Wednesday.
On the 23rd [February] at breakfast got sick with measles—was put to bed. Aleksei [got sick] during the day, and Anya too. The ear[ache] went away slowly. The next day Tat.[iana] got sick, [we] lay down together. Al. came by during the day in his bed—it was dark. My T° reached 40,3. Mama is with us all the time. Shvybz got sick on the 2nd [of] M.[arch]—Maria [on] the 7th. On the 27th or 28th Febr. Lili Dehn arrived here and is still living in the Red Room.

[Olga's diary abruptly ends on March 15, 1917. Perhaps out of depression or other reasons, she never recorded in her diary any further events. She did write numerous letters to friends and relatives from exile, first from the Siberian city of Tobolsk, and later from Ekaterinburg. From here on, others take over to finish her story.]

—

From the memoirs of Anna Vyrubova (March 1917):
On the first evening after the transfer of the palace into the hands of the revolutionary soldiers we heard shooting under the windows. *Kamerder* Volkov came with the report that the soldiers entertained themselves in the park by hunting the Emperor's favorite wild goats. We lived through terrible hours. While handfuls of drunken and arrogant soldiers strolled through the palace, the Empress was destroying all her dear letters and diaries and in my room, with her own hands burned six cases of her letters to me, not wanting them to end up in the hands of these wicked people.

—

From the diary of Nicholas II:
16th March. Thursday.
Clear frosty day. Walked in the morning. Maria and Anastasia are [feeling] the same, in bed in a dark room and coughing a lot; they have bronchitis. Walked and worked during the day. In the evening sat at Anya's and then at Benkendorf's.

17th March. Friday.
The same [kind of] sunny day. Walked from 11 o'cl. until 11 1/2 o'cl. Maria and Anastasia's temp. went up and down alternatively, and also [they were] vomiting. Took a long walk during the day and worked; finished the path by the old gazebo with Valya D. In the evening stopped by Anya's and Lilly Dehn's.

18th March. Saturday.
A gray day and a warm spell; in the morning during my walk there was some wet snow. During the day Maria had [tem-

perature of] 40.9 and occasional delirium, in the evening it went down to 39.3; Anastasia, during the day—37.8, in the evening—39.3. Worked a bit during the day. At 6 1/2 went to *vsenoshnaya* with Olga and Tatiana. Spent the evening with the family and [we] dispersed early to rest.

19th March. Sunday.
Bright day. At 11 o'cl. went to *obednya* with Olga, Tatiana and Aleksei. Maria's and Anastasia's temp. went down to normal, and only in the evening Maria's went up a little. Went for a walk at 2 o'clock, walked, worked and enjoyed the weather. Returned home at 4 1/2. Sat with the children for a long time, and [we] were at Anya's and others' in the evening.

—

From the memoirs of Anna Vyrubova:
   On 19 March I received a note from the Empress that Maria Nikolaevna is dying and asking for me. The messenger told me that Anastasia Nikolevna is also very sick; both had pneumonia, and the latter also became deaf due to the ear infection. . . . For a minute I fought with feeling of pity for the dying Maria Nikolaevna and fear for myself, but the first prevailed and I got up, got dressed and Kotzeba pushed me in a wheelchair through the upper hallway to the children's quarters, whom I had not seen for a whole month. A happy exclamation from Aleksei and the older girls made me forget all. We ran to each other, hugged and cried. Then I tiptoed to Maria Nikolaevna. She was lying there, white like linen, her eyes, naturally large, seemed even larger, temperature was 40.9, she breathed oxygen. When she saw me, she made some attempts to pick up her head and started to cry, repeating: "Anya, Anya." I stayed with her until she fell asleep.

—

From the diary of Nicholas II:
20th March. Monday.
Apparently Maria's and Anastasia's illness broke, the temp. remained normal; they are weak and slept all day, of course with breaks. Walked from 11 o'cl. Lots of [snow is] thawing. Worked a little during the day. Sat at Anya's in the evening.

—

From the memoirs of Anna Vyrubova:
    The only thing that he [Nicholas II] wished for, and was ready to beg his enemies for without losing his pride—was not to be exiled from Russia. "Let me live here with my family and be the simplest of peasants, earning his bread,"—He said,—"send us to the most safe corner of our motherland, but let us stay in Russia." This was the one and only time when I saw the Russian Tsar so absolutely crushed by the events; on all the subsequent days he was calm.
    Daily, I watched from the window at how he shoveled snow from the path, right across from my window. The path went around a meadow and Prince Dolgoruky and the Emperor shoveled the snow towards each other; the soldiers and some recruits walked around them. Often, the Emperor looked around at the window where the Empress and I were sitting, and undetected by others smiled at us or waved his hand.

—

From the memoirs of V. I. Chebotareva:
March 1917.
Complete disarray at the infirmary. . . . The Sisters volunteered to switch to soldiers' food rations, when the committee protested about the extra butter they were getting, the civil zeal has cooled off, and the Red Cross made remarks

even to Vera Ignatievna: nothing that has not been made into law can be carried out.

—

From the memoirs of Alexander Kerensky:[14]

When the Alexander Palace was put under my control, the first thing I did was to look for a commandant, a person who I was familiar with for a long time, who deserved utmost trust, [who was] controlled, calm, with firm character and the nobility of a knight. The first commandant I chose, Colonel Korovichenko, occasionally would exasperate the imperial family with [his] starcs and blatant crudeness, [which are] often common to shy people.

—

From the diary of Nicholas II:
21st March. Tuesday.
Kerensky, the current Minister of Justice, showed up unexpectedly today, walked through all the rooms, wanted to see us, spoke with me for about five minutes, introduced the new commandant of the palace and then left. He ordered the arrest of poor Anya and for her to be taken to the city along with Lillie Dehn. This happened between 3 and 4 o'cl. while I was taking a walk. The weather was awful and matched our mood! Maria and Anastasia slept almost the entire day. After dinner the four of us, with O. and T. spent a quiet evening.

—

From the memoirs of Alexander Kerensky:
I remember well my first visit to the imperial family. This was sometime in mid-March, during my first inspection of the recently appointed palace sentries. . . . I asked the *uber-*

14. Head of the Provisional Government.

gofmarshall Count Benkendorf to warn the Tsar of my wish to see him and the Empress. The old aristocrat with a monocle promised to announce me to His Majesty based on etiquette. He returned soon, and formally announced: "His Majesty has kindly agreed to admit you". . . . To be honest I will admit that I was not at all neutral about my first meeting with Nicholas II. There were so many cruel and awful events associated with his name in the past, that I was afraid to lose control and not be able to get over my secret negative feelings. . . . Through the door opened by Benkendorf I immediately saw the entire imperial family behind the door to the adjacent room. They gathered a little to the left of the door, behind a round table by the window, assembling into a confused nervous little bunch.

From this group, a man of medium height with military manners stepped forward, and with a calm weak smile came towards me. This was the Emperor. . . . With an analogous smile I stepped towards him, extended my hand in the usual manner [and] introduced myself: "Kerensky," as is normally done at first meetings. Nicholas responded by shaking my hand, and immediately got over his discomfort, smiled again and took me over to his family. The daughters and little Tsesarevich focused on me with obvious curiosity. Alexandra Fedorovna, standing in one spot rigidly, unfriendly, haughty, controlled, slowly unwillingly extended her hand. I was not dying to shake it; our palms barely touched each other.

—

From the memoirs of Anna Vyrubova:

The next day, my last day in Tsarskoe Selo, I went to see the children again and we were happy to be together. Their Majesties were having breakfast in the children's rooms and were calm, since Maria and Anastasia Nikolaevnas felt better.

On the morning of 21st of March I was nervous, I found out that the soldiers were not allowing Kotzeba into the palace, likely due to his humane treatment of the captives. . . It was a dark and cold day, the wind was howling. In the morning I wrote a note to the Empress, asking her not to wait until midday and stop by my room in the morning. She responded for me to come to the children's room at two o'clock, as right now their doctors were in there. Lillie Dehn had breakfast with me. I stayed in bed. About one [o'clock] there was sudden pandemonium in the hallway, and I heard fast footsteps. I felt chilled and felt that they were coming for me.

At first one of our men, Yevseyev, ran in with a note from the Empress: "Kerensky is making rounds of our rooms,— God is with us." After a minute Lillie, who was calming me down, tore from her seat and ran off. The messenger reported that Kerensky is coming. Surrounded by officers, into the room walked an arrogant looking little man with a clean-shaved face, hollered that he is the minister and that I had to get ready to go with him to Petrograd, right now. . .

In a minute some military types crowded around my door, I got dressed quickly and having written a note to the Empress, sent her my large icon of the Savior. I, in turn, received two icons on a shoestring from the Empress and the Emperor with their signatures on the other side.

In tears I appealed to the commandant Korovichenko to allow me to say goodbye to the Empress. I saw the Emperor from the window, when he passed by on his walk, almost running, [he] was in a hurry, but they did not let him in. . . . I tried not to notice anything and focused my gaze on my beloved Empress, whose footman Volkov rolled her in a wheelchair. Tatiana Nikolaevna was escorting her [the Empress]. From afar I saw that the Empress and Tatiana Nikolaevna were sobbing; the good Volkov was weeping too.

One long embrace, we had time to exchange rings, Tatiana Nikolaevna took my wedding band. The Empress, through [her] sobs said, pointing to the heavens: "There and in God we will always be together." I almost don't remember how they tore us apart. Volkov kept repeating: "Anna Alexandrovna, no one—but God!" When I looked at the faces of our persecutors, I saw that they were in tears too. They had to almost carry me to the motor car.

—

From the diary of Nicholas II:
22nd March. Wednesday.
There was a storm during the night and masses of snow. The day remained sunny and quiet. Olga and Tatiana went outside for the first time, and sat on the round balcony while I was walking. After breakfast I worked a lot. The younger ones slept a lot and felt well. Spent the entire time together.

23rd March. Thursday.
A bright day after 2 o'cl and a warm spell. Took a short walk in the morning. Took inventory of my things and books and started to put aside everything that I want to bring with me if we have to go to England. After breakfast walked with Olga and Tatiana and worked in the garden. Spent the evening as usual.

24th March. Friday.
A nice quiet day. Walked in the morning. During the day Maria and Anastasia were transferred to the playroom. Successfully worked with Valya D.; now almost all the paths are clear [of snow]. At 6 1/2 went to *vsenoshnaya* with O. and T. In the evening read Chekhov aloud.

25th March. Annunciation.

Spent this holiday in strange circumstances—arrested in our own home and without even a remote possibility of contact with Mama and with our [relatives and friends]! At 11 o'cl. went to *obednya* with O. and T. After breakfast walked and worked with them on the little island. The weather was overcast. At 6 1/2 went to *vsenoshnaya* and returned with pussy willows. Anastasia got up and walked around the rooms upstairs.

—

From the memoirs of Alexander Kerensky:

The life of the imperial family at the Alexander Palace was somewhat restricted:

1. The members of the imperial family, the courtiers and servants who remained with them, were forbidden to leave the palace grounds or to have any contact with the outside world.

2. The prisoners kept their privilege of moving around freely inside the palace, but outside walks were only allowed in the fenced in part of the park with the guards' supervision.

3. The imperial family and the suite were allowed to go to church services at the palace chapel.

4. Persons not residing at the palace were only allowed in with my permission.

5. All the correspondence addressed to the detainees was examined by the commandant.

6. The palace and park were under constant supervision by the armed guards.

7. The guards were observed by the outer patrol, while the inner guard inevitably answered to the commandant appointed by the Provisional Government.

With the exception of these restrictions, the imperial family's life in the palace was as usual.

—

From the diary of Nicholas II:
27th March. Monday.
Began *govet'*[15] but it did not start out joyfully. After *obednya*
Kerensky arrived and asked us to limit our contact with the
children during meals and to sit separately; supposedly he
needs this in order to calm down the infamous Soviet of the
Workers' and Soldiers' Deputies! We had to submit in order
to avoid violence.

Took a walk with Tatiana. Olga got ill again with a sore
throat. The rest feel well. At 9.45 went down to my rooms,
Tatiana sat with me until 10 1/2 o'cl. Then I read, had some
tea, took a bath and went to sleep on my cot!

28th March. Tuesday.
Slept very well. The weather was warm, the road became even
worse because of it; took a walk. At 11 o'cl. went to *obednya*.
Olga's throat continues to hurt, temp. rose up to 39.4, how
tiresome—she only recently recovered from the measles.
Walked and worked on the little island with T. At 6 1/2 o'cl.
Anastasia went to the service with us. Spent the evening with
Tatiana again and spent the night in my room.

29th March. Wednesday.
A nice warm day. Got up at 9 1/2 o'cl. as I did not sleep well.
Took a walk before *obednya*. The service is [now] conducted
in the campaign church [by] Father Afanasiy Belyaev, due to
the illness of our priest F. Vasilyev, the deacon, lector and
four choristers, who were excellent at their duties. Such a
shame that all the children can't go to church with us! Took
a walk with T. and worked for a long time with her on the

15. Fasting and attending divine services during the Holy Week.

little island; two of the guards also helped us. After dinner spent the evening together until 10 o'cl., and then Tatiana sat with me. Went to bed early.

30th March. Thursday.
It was very windy [which] blew away the clouds during the day. At 10 o'cl. went to *obednya*, where a lot of our people received holy communion. Took a short walk with Tatiana; today they had the funeral for the "victims of the revolution" in our park across from the center of the Alexander Palace, not far from the Chinese [pavilion]. One could hear the sounds of the funeral march and the *Marseillaise*.

—

From the memoirs of Anna Vyrubova:
The Empress and the children were constantly awaiting N. Sabdin [*sic*—should be Sablin], their closest friend, but he did not appear, and others ran too. The loyal teachers of Aleksei Nikolaevich, Mr. Gilliard and Mr. Gibbe[s], some servants, all the nannies, who announced that they served in the good times and will never abandon the family now, both doctors, E. Botkin and V. Derevenko. In general, all of Her Majesty's people, all to the last person . . . stayed.

—

From the diary of Nicholas II:
1st April. Saturday.
Forgot to mention that yesterday we said goodbye to 46 of our servants who were finally released from the Alexander Palace to [go to] their families in Petrograd. The weather was nice with a strong southern wind. Walked until breakfast. During the day started to break the ice as usual by the bridge over a stream; [with us] worked Tatiana, Valya and

Nagorny.[16] Took a nap until dinner. Gave each other gifts of [Easter] eggs and photos. At 11 1/2 went to the beginning of the midnight service.

2nd April. Holy Easter Sunday.
Morning service and *obednya* ended at one 40. . . . The day was bright, really festive. Took a walk in the morning. Before breakfast exchanged triple kisses with all the servants, and Alix gave them china eggs which we had in stock. Altogether there were 135 people [present]. During the day started to work by the bridge, but soon a large crowd of onlookers gathered behind the lattice fence—we were forced to leave and spend the rest of the time bored in the garden. Aleksei and Anastasia went outside for the first time. At 7 o'cl. there was an evening service in the playroom. After dinner [we] dispersed at 10 o'cl.; read to Tatiana aloud in my room. Went to bed early.

—

From the memoirs of V. I. Chebotareva:
April 1917.
    We know very little about the prisoners [imperial family at the Alexander Palace], although get some occasional letters. Varvara Afanasievna got two from Tatiana, and also Rita [got a letter]. In the first one, Tatianochka wrote: "I heard that the infirmary has been transferred to a new building. Will try to ensure that the dishware we ordered is delivered (was done yesterday). Send our things. [This] letter will most likely be opened by local censors."
    Sent [them] their uniforms, albums, camera and the icon from the dining room, which we all purchased—the last

16. Klementy Nagorny was Aleksei's sailor nanny, who voluntarily went into exile with the imperial family and was murdered by the revolutionaries.

regard from the infirmary. At the time, Shakh Bagov chose it. Yesterday, Tatiana wrote again: "Dear Varvara Afanasievna, sending things, shirts, pillows, some of the books. Please tell darling Bibi that we love and kiss her tenderly. What are Mitya and Volodya up to? And how about Valentina Ivanovna and Grisha?"[17]

In the evening a postcard [addressed to] my name was delivered: "Christ has risen! We kiss darling Valentina Ivanovna thrice. Sisters Alexandra, Olga, Tatiana." Vera Ignatievna feels that we cannot each respond, in order not to create the perception of "faction." Rita should respond for all. The commandant says that we can write. Is Vera Ignatievna right? Can we not exchange a Christian greeting on such a revered holiday?

Olga has angina, fever 39.9. Aleksei Nikolaevich is lying down, bruised his arm, bleeding again. The mother is always with the children, the father evidently is separated, seldom sees [them].

They say that when Kerensky arrived, Aleksei Nikolaevich came out and to the question: "Do you have all you need?" [he] answered: "Yes, but I am so bored, I love soldiers."—[Response was] "Look at how many of them are in the park."—"No, these are not the same, these are not going to the front, I love those others." [I] do not guarantee the veracity [of the above story].

———

From the diary of Nicholas II:
10th April. Monday.
The day stayed cool. Aleksei got a little bit of a sore throat and was put to bed. During the day worked with Tatiana between the bridges. Spent the evening as usual.

17. Chebotareva and her son.

11th April. Tuesday.
Once again a wonderful day. During the day Alix finally came out with us for a walk. Nagorny pushed her in a wheelchair. She watched as we worked on the ice. The sun warmed [us] wonderfully. Read before dinner. Alix requested a *vsenoshnaya* upstairs for the children. Sat downstairs in my room with Tatiana until 11 o'cl.

12th April. Wednesday.
Cold windy day. Took a half hour walk and then sat with the children while Alix was at *obednya.* Kerensky came during the day and distracted me from my work on the ice. At first he spoke with Alix, then with me. Read after tea. In the evening we sat upstairs, had tea together and slept altogether too.

—

From the memoirs of Anna Vyrubova:
  The parlor maid told me how they [the imperial family] spent the summer, how at one point Their Majesties were separated from each other and [were] only allowed to speak [to each other] during dinner and breakfast in the presence of the officers.
  The Revolutionary government tried with all their might to implicate the Empress in treason, etc., but they were not successful. They hated her a lot more than the Emperor. When their accusations did not find any proof they once again were allowed to be together.

—

From the diary of Nicholas II:
19th April. Wednesday.
The weather was the same as yesterday but a little warmer. From 12 o'cl. until breakfast time sat with Aleksei at his

Russian history lessons. Took a walk with him and Tatiana during the day. For the first time the entire family had dinner at the same table—Olga and Maria recovered at last.

22nd April. Saturday.
An excellent spring day. Took a walk with Aleksei from 11 o'cl. until 12 o'cl.; he played on the island[18] while the marksmen stood on the other side and watched. During the day worked on the same spot. The sun was very warm. At 6 1/2 went to *vsenoshnaya* with the entire family. Before dinner Alix got modest gifts from the "prisoners," an appropriate term of Maria's. In the evening read aloud.

23rd April. Sunday.
Wonderful weather for dear Alix's name day. Before *obednya*, the ladies and gentlemen residing at the palace, and also our people, came with good wishes. Had breakfast as usual upstairs. At 2 o'clock the entire family went out to the garden. Worked on the lake around the "Children's" island; broke up and dispersed all the ice. Returned home at 4 1/2 o'clock. Read in my room before dinner and in the evening, aloud. From 9 o'cl. it started to rain.

9th June. Friday.
Exactly three months since I arrived from Mogilev and that we have been under arrest. It's hard not to [be able to] get any news from dear mama, the rest [of it] I am indifferent to. Today is an even hotter day; 25° in the shade, in the sun 36°. Again there was a strong burning smell. After my walk [I] tutored Aleksei in history in my new study, as it was cooler there. Worked nicely in the same spot. Alix did not go out.

18. Children's Island in Alexander Park.

Before dinner the five of us took a walk.

—

From the memoirs of Alexander Kerensky:
This peaceful court life was only a temporary illusion. More than once the instated order was tossed around by the increasingly strong collisions with the revolutionary waves. The curious passers-by surrounded the park, eyeing them through the fence, especially on Sundays and holidays. When they saw the tsar taking his walk, they booed and whistled. When the imperial daughters and other women who lived at the palace appeared, they were met with various playful comments.

The guards inside the park demonstratively followed instructions, walking just behind the captives, treating them insolently, in all sorts of ways of demonstrating their displeasure with the failed emperor.

—

From the diary of Nicholas II:
10th June. Saturday.
During the night and during the day until 3 o'cl. it continued to be swelteringly hot and muggy. Took a long walk in the morning. Had breakfast, same as yesterday in the children's dining room. During the day worked in the same spot.

A rainstorm passed in the distance, there were a few drops of rain. Fortunately it got cooler. At 6 1/2 went to *vsenoshnaya*. In the evening, around 11 o'cl. we heard a shot from the garden, after 1/4 hour the chief guard asked [permission] to come in and explained that a guard did shoot, because he thought that he saw a red light signal from one of the children's bedroom windows. Having checked the location of the electric light and seeing the movement of Anastasia's head, [who was] sitting by the window, one of the unter-of.[ficers] who came in with him, realized what happened and they left, having apologized.

—

From the memoirs of Alexander Kerensky:
Once, early in the revolution, when the imperial children were sick with measles, the family gathered in one room to read. Immediately, the guards ran in with a warning that there were light signals coming from the windows of the palace, and that something needs to be done. At first everyone was confused. Then there was an explanation. One of the grand duchesses, Tatiana or Olga, sat between the window and a lamp, dreamily nodding her head, which caused the light behind the girl to dim and then to glow again.

—

From the diary of Nicholas II:
8th July. Saturday.
Beautiful day; took a walk with pleasure. After breakfast found out from Count Benkendorf that we are not being sent to the Crimea but to one of the far away provinces, three or four days' worth trip east! But where exactly they won't tell us, and even the commandant doesn't know. And we really expected a long stay in Livadia!

Cut down and felled a huge pine tree on the glade path. There was a brief warm rain. In the evening I am reading "A Study in Scarlet" by Conan Doyle, aloud.

—

From the memoirs of Alexander Kerensky:
To demonstrate this awful tragedy of the imperial family in the truest light, we must remember this: when the

Provisional Government announced the decision to arrest the tsar and he chose Tsarskoe Selo as the place of his captivity, it was thought that this situation would be in place for a short duration. Transfer to England seemed so close that on 7 (23) March the British consulate, George Buchanan, had sent a verbal message to the Minister of Foreign Affairs of the Provisional Government, P. N. Milyukov that His Majesty the King and His Majesty's government are happy to offer refuge in England to the former Russian Emperor. There were no exterior obstacles to the Tsar's departure. Interior difficulties arose. In the general chaos which reigned in the early days of the revolution, the government was not yet fully in control of the administrative machine. For example, the railroads were freely ruled by various unions and advisories. There was no opportunity to bring the Tsar to Murmansk without exposing him to unavoidable and very serious dangers. On the way, he could end up in the hands of the "revolutionary masses" and wind up not in England but in St Peter and Paul Fortress, or even worse, in Kronstadt . . .

But in specific English circles, especially among the liberals and laborites, the intention of the British government to offer hospitality to the former Russian Tsar was met very coldly. . . . On 10th April (new style) the newspapers released a semi-official statement of the British Ministry of the Foreign Affairs which could be viewed as a retraction. . . . "The British government does not insist on the offer made earlier to provide a refuge to the imperial family." What does "does not insist on the offer made earlier" mean? One would think that the British government persistently negotiated with the Russian Provisional Government about the transfer of the imperial family to England, and not being able to get an agreement were forced to retreat from their noble intention to save the cousin of their own king and the favorite

granddaughter of Queen Victoria from the horrible revolutionaries.

In reality, it was the complete opposite. 6 (19) March, the
Minister of Foreign Affairs P. N. Milyukov notified Sir
George Buchanan of the Provisional Government's intention
to send the former Tsar and his family to England. After
three days the British government, in response to three
telegrams, had agreed to accept the imperial family. What
happened next? Soon after a legend emerged in which the
English government "never refused to offer an invitation."

—

From the diary of Nicholas II:
10th July. Monday.
[Took a] morning walk around the entire park. During the
day cut down four dry pine trees and cut them up right there
for firewood. Returned home exactly at 5 o'cl. Read a lot.
Before dinner Olga received gifts.[19]

11th July. Tuesday.
Took a walk with Aleksei in the morning. At our return
found out about Kerensky's arrival. During the conversation
he mentioned our probable departure for the south, due to
the proximity of T. Selo to the restless capital.

In honor of Olga's name day went to *molebna*. After breakfast worked nicely in the usual spot; cut down two pine
trees—getting close to seventy sawed trees. Finished reading
the third part of the Merezhkovsky trilogy "Peter"; well written, but makes a difficult impression.

—

19. For Olga's name day.

From the memoirs of Alexander Kerensky:
One day some automobile hit the fence of the Palace Park. Naturally the entire Tsarskoe Selo screamed treason: someone was trying to kidnap the tsar! The car was planning to tear through to the [palace] entrance! So we had to post completely useless sentries at the broken fence.

—

From the diary of Nicholas II:
12th July. Wednesday.
The day was windy and cold—only 10°. Took a walk with all the daughters. . . . All of us were thinking of the impending trip; the departure from here seems so strange after 4 months of captivity!

13th July. Thursday.
In the last few days bad news has been coming from the southwestern front. After our offense at Galich, a lot of regiments [were] infected by the ignoble defeatist preaching, [and] not only refused to move forward but in some areas retreated without even any pressure from the enemy. Taking advantage of this beneficial, for them, circumstance the Germans and the Austrians broke through southern Galicia despite low military strength, which may force the entire southwestern front to retreat east. Complete disgrace and despair! Today the Provisional Government finally announced that capital punishment has been instated against those on the military arena who are convicted of treason. I hope that these measures are not too late.

The day stayed warm and overcast. Worked on the same spot on the side of the glade. Cut down three and cut up two felled timber logs. Slowly starting to pack clothes and books.

19th July. Wednesday.

Three years ago Germany declared war on us; it seems like a whole lifetime ago, these three years! Lord, help and save Russia!

It was very hot. Took a walk with T., M. and A. Once again [with us was] the entire convoy of guards from the 3rd regiment. Worked on the same spot. Felled four trees and finished the pine trees which were felled yesterday. Now I am reading Merezhkovsky's novel *Alexander I.*

—

From the memoirs of Alexander Kerensky:

We could wait no longer. We had to send the imperial family somewhere farther out, to some quiet place which would be hard to find in Russia at that time. . . . I started looking for an appropriate place. At first I was going to send them somewhere in central Russia, say to the estate of one of the grand dukes, Mikhail Alexandrovich or Nikolai Mikhailovich, with whom I even discussed such a project. Immediately it became clear that the peasants did not feel very friendly towards this idea. The very fact of their transfer to those areas . . . through densely populated regions was impossible. The Tsar wanted very much to go to the Crimea, and all his hopes focused on that, possibly even more so than their departure to England. One by one all his relatives headed there [to the Crimea], the Dowager Empress being one of the first. But the idea of the congregation of the former members of the deposed imperial dynasty already started to make everyone nervous. Besides that there was the unanswered question—how to transport the imperial train through all of Russia from north to south.

Why did I eventually choose Tobolsk, which was not that much farther than the Crimea? Some monarchists insisted (and perhaps still do until this day) that the only reason for this choice was the wish to "avenge the Tsar with the same coin," by sending him to Siberia, where in the past all revolutionaries were sent. In reality, it was possible to get to Tobolsk via northern route, passing through the densely populated regions. As far as revenge, why would we want to organize transport to Tobolsk when the Peter and Paul Fortress, or better yet, Kronstadt, were right nearby.

I preferred to choose Tobolsk exclusively because it was indeed isolated, especially during the winter. The town with well-to-do, satisfied residents, far away from railroads . . . and [it] lacked any active proletariat. In addition I knew about their superb winter climate and a rather appropriate governor's house, where the imperial family could live in comfort.

—

From the diary of Nicholas II:
29th July. Saturday.
The same beautiful weather. During the morning walk, while passing by the gates on the way to the orangerie, we noticed a guard sleeping in the grass. *Unter-officer* who was escorting us came over and took away his rifle.

During the day we cut down 9 trees and sawed up one pine tree—all right by the road. It was humid and cloudy, and thunder was heard, but the sky cleared up towards the evening. After *vsenoshnaya* Aleksei got gifts.

Cleaned up and packed my things, so now the rooms look so empty.

30th July. Sunday.
Today dear Aleksei turned 13 years old. May the Lord grant him health, patience, strength of character and body in these difficult times!

Went to *obednya*, and after breakfast to *molebna*, where we brought the *Znamenie* Madonna icon. It felt especially nice to pray to her holy image with all our people. The marksmen of the 3rd regiment brought it and carried it away across the garden.

—

From the memoirs of Alexander Kerensky:
When finally the approximate departure date was confirmed, I spoke with the emperor during one of my regular visits to Tsarskoe Selo, described the difficult situation in St Petersburg, and proposed that they prepare for departure. Of course I notified him of the British government's refusal, but did not confirm where they will be taken only advised that they bring warm clothing. He listened to me very attentively. . . . Our eyes met. Possibly in my eyes he read reassurance: the tsar, who rarely trusted anyone, who lived through betrayal from his close associates, now expressed trust towards the person whom his wife only recently wished to see hanged.

—

From the diary of Nicholas II:
31st July. Monday.
The last day of our stay at Tsarskoe Selo. The weather was beautiful. Worked in the same spot during the day; cut down three trees and sawed up yesterday's [trees]. After dinner waited for the appointed hour of departure, which kept being delayed. Unexpectedly Kerensky arrived and announced that Misha[20] will be coming soon. And in fact, around 10 1/2 dear Misha came in, escorted by Ker.[ensky] and the chief of the

20. Grand Duke Michael Alexandrovich (1878–1918), youngest brother of Nicholas II.

guards. It was so nice to see each other, but it was awkward to talk in front of outsiders.

When he left, the sentry marksmen started to drag our luggage to the circular hall. The Benkendorfs, ladies-in-waiting, chambermaids and our people were there too. We paced back and forth, waiting for the trucks to arrive. The secret about our departure was kept to a point where the motor [car]s and the train were ordered after our appointed departure time. . . . Aleksei wanted to sleep; he lay down then got up. A few times there was a false alarm, we put on our coats, came out on the balcony and returned to the hall. It got light [outside].

We had tea and finally at 5 o'cl. Kerensky appeared and said that we can go now. We climbed into two motors and went to the Alexander station. Climbed into the train at the crossing. Some kind of a cavalry team rode astride near us, all the way from the park. We were met by: I. Tatishev and two commissars from the government in order to escort us to Tobolsk.

The sunrise was beautiful, at which point we started the trip towards Petrograd and via connecting path came out onto the Northern line. Departed T.[arskoe] S.[elo] at 6.10 in the morning.

—

From the memoirs of Anna Vyrubova:

A few days before their departure to Siberia, I got a short letter from the Empress and a box of my gold jewelry that she saved during my arrest. . . .

After their departure to Siberia, the little parlor maid once again visited me. She described how Kerensky arranged their trip and spent hours at the palace. How difficult it was for Their Majesties. He commanded that they all be ready to leave at midnight.

The Imperial captives sat in the circular hall from 12 o'clock until 6 in the morning, dressed in traveling clothes. At 5 o'clock in morning one of the loyal lackeys was not afraid to bring them tea, which perked them up a little. Aleksei Nikolaevich was feeling faint. They departed from the palace with dignity, completely calm, as if they were leaving for their holiday at the Crimea or Finland. Even the revolutionary newspapers could not find fault with anything.

—

EXILE

—

From the diary of Nicholas II:
1st August.
Arranged ourselves in a nice sleeping car in the International Society [train]. Went to bed at 7.45 and slept until 9.15 o'cl. It was very stuffy and dusty; 26° in the car. Took a walk during the day with our marksmen, picked flowers and berries. [We] eat in the train restaurant, the kitchen feeds us very well, Eastern-Chinese food and etc.

2nd August.
Took a walk before Vyatka, same weather and dust. By commandant's request had to close window shades at all stations; tiresome and foolish!

3rd August.
Passed Perm at 4 o'cl. and walked in the Kungur suburbs along the Sylva river, in a very beautiful valley.

4th August.
Having passed the Urals, felt a significant coolness. Passed Ekaterinburg very early in the morning. All these days the second train with marksmen would catch up to us—we greeted [each other] like old acquaintances.

Rode incredibly slowly, in order to arrive in Tyumen late, at 11 1/2 o'cl. There, the train arrived almost next to the wharf, so we only had to walk down to the ship. Ours is called *Rus.* They started to load our things, which continued through the night. Poor Aleksei went to bed God knows when again! Banging and pounding lasted all night and did not let me sleep. Departed from Tyumen around 6 o'cl.

5th August.
Cruising down the river Tur. Slept a lot. Alix, Aleksei and I each have a cabin with no facilities, all the daughters are together in a five-bed [cabin], the suite is close by in the hallway; farther towards the bow is a nice cafeteria and a small cabin with a piano. The second class is under us, and all the marksmen of the 1st regiment who were on the train with us are downstairs in the back. Walked around upstairs [deck] all day, enjoying the air. The weather was overcast, but quiet and warm. In front of us is a ship and behind is another ship with the marksmen of the 2nd and 4th regiments and with the rest of the luggage. Stopped twice to load firewood. At night it got cold. Our kitchen is right here on the ship. Everyone went to bed early.

6th August.
Cruising down the Tobol [river]. Got up late, as I slept badly due to the general noise, whistles, stops, etc. During the night, entered Tobol from Tur. The river is wider, and the shore is higher. The morning was cool, and during the day it got really warm when the sun came out.

Forgot to mention that yesterday before dinner we passed by Pokrovskoye village,—Grigori's hometown.[21] Walked and sat all day on the deck. At 6 1/2 arrived in Tobolsk, although saw it an hour and 1/4 earlier.

There was a big crowd gathered on the shore,—this means that they know about our arrival. I remembered the view of the cathedral and the house on the mountain. As soon as the ship docked, they started to unload the luggage. Valya, the commissar and the commandant went off to look over the houses appointed for us and our suite. When they returned we found out that the buildings are empty, without any furniture, dirty and we cannot move in. Therefore [we stayed] on the ship and started waiting for them to bring back the luggage needed for sleeping.

Had supper, joked about the incredible incompetency of these people who cannot even arrange a dwelling and went to bed early.

7th August. Monday.
Slept very well; woke up to rain and cold. Decided to remain on the ship. Some storms passed, but the weather got better by one o'clock. The crowd was still standing at the docks, their feet in the water, and [they] only ran to shelter when it rained. In both houses they are hastily cleaning and getting the rooms into presentable shape. All of us, including the marksmen, wanted to go somewhere farther down the river. Had breakfast at one, dinner at 8 o'cl., the kitchen staff is already cooking in the house, and someone brings our food from there. Walked around our cabins with the children all evening. The weather was cold due to N-W wind.

21. This was very significant to the imperial family because allegedly Rasputin predicted that they would one day visit his village in person.

8th August. Tuesday.
Slept very well and got up at 9 o'cl. The morning was bright, later got windy, and again got hit with several storms. After breakfast went up the river Irtysh, about 10 *versts*. Docked on the right shore and went out to walk. Walked by some hedges and having crossed the creek, we went up a high bank from where a beautiful view opened up.

The ship came to pick us up and we headed back to Tobolsk. Arrived at 6 o'cl., [docked] at a different wharf. Took a bath before dinner, for the first time since July 31st. Thanks to that [I] slept wonderfully.

9th August. Wednesday.
The weather still wonderfully warm. The suite spent the morning in town as usual. Maria had fever, Aleksei had some pains in his left arm.

Before breakfast I remained upstairs the whole time, enjoying the sun. At 2 1/2 our ship moved to the other side and they started loading coal, while we went for a walk. Joy [Aleksei's pet spaniel] was bitten by a snake.

It was too hot to walk. Came back to the ship at 4 1/2 and returned to the old spot. The residents were boating and passed by us. The marksmen from our convoy *Kormiletz* moved into their town residences.

10th August. Thursday.
Woke up to rotten weather—rainy and windy. Maria was in bed with fever, and Aleksei got an earache in addition to pains in the arm!

The day was most boring, without a walk or anything to do. At 5 o'cl. the weather got better.

11th August. Friday.
Aleksei slept very little, he moved to Alix's room for the

night. His ear got better, the arm still hurts a bit. Maria is better. The day was calm.

Walked around upstairs all morning. During the day went up the river Tobol. Docked at the left bank, walked down the road and returned along the river with all sorts of difficulties, of the amusing sort. At 6 o'cl. arrived in Tobolsk and with a loud crack approached the ship *Tovarpar*, breaking our side plating on it. During the day it was really hot.

12th August. Saturday.
Again an excellent day without sun, but very warm. In the morning walked around the deck and read there too until breakfast. Maria and Aleksei got up and went outside for fresh air during the day. At 3 o'clock went down Irtysh and docked at the base of a high bank, which we have wanted to get to. Immediately climbed up there with the marksmen and then sat for a long time on a plain low stool, a wonderful view.

13th August. Sunday.
Got up early, and packed our last things immediately. At 10 1/2, I and the children went down to the shore with the commandant and the officers and walked to our new residence. Looked around the entire house, from the top to the attic. Occupied the second floor, the dining room is downstairs. At 12 o'cl. [had a] *moleben* service, and the priest baptized all the rooms with holy water. Had breakfast and dinner with our people. Went to see the house where the suite will be staying. Many rooms are still not ready and look unattractive.

Then went to the so-called garden—terrible kitchen garden, looked over the kitchen and the guard room. Everything looks old and dilapidated. Unpacked my things in the study and bathroom, which is half mine and half Aleksei's. Spent the evening together, played bezique with Nastenka.

14th August. Monday.
After yesterday's rainstorm, the weather was cold and rainy before dinner, with a strong wind. Organized photographs from 1890/1891 sailing trips all day. I purposely brought them with us, in order to organize them at leisure. Said good-bye to Makarov—the commissar who was leaving for Moscow. Took a walk in the little garden, the children played on the new swings. Spent the evening with everyone.

15th August. Tuesday.
Since they do not let us go outside and we cannot get to church right now, at 11 o'cl. there was an *obednitza*[22] service in the hall. After breakfast spent almost two hours in the garden, Alix too. The weather was warm, and around 5 o'cl. the sun came out; sat on the balcony until 6 1/2 o'cl. Continued organizing photographs from the distant seafaring days.

16th August. Wednesday.
An excellent warm day. Now I have tea with all the children every morning. Spent an hour's worth of time in the so-called garden and most of the day on the balcony, was warmed by the sun all day. Before tea, puttered around in the little garden, two hours on the swings and with the bonfire.

17th August. Thursday.
Magnificent day; 19° in the shade, 36° on the balcony. Aleksei had pains in his arm. Spent an hour in the morning in the garden, and during the day—two hours. Yesterday started to read "L'ile enchantee." In the evening played dominos: Alix, Tatiana, Botkin and I. At teatime there was a big rainstorm. Moonlit night.

22. An abbreviated *obednya* service.

18th August. Friday.
The morning was gray and cold, the sun came out around one, and the day became really nice. In the morning, Rita Khitrovo, who came from Petrograd, appeared in the street, and went to see Nastenka Hendr.[ikova]. This was sufficient for them to search her home in the evening. Devil knows what this is!

19th August. Saturday.
Due to yesterday's incident, Nastenka is no longer allowed to walk in the streets for a few days, and poor Rita Khitrovo has to go back on the evening ship!
The weather stayed lovely with hot sun. Sat in the garden for an hour in the morning, and during the day—two hours. Set up a hanging bar for myself there. Started the book: *The Scarlet Pimpernel*.

20th August. Sunday.
Ideal weather: during the day the temp. reaches 21° in the shade. At 11 o'cl. *obednitza* service in the hall. Found work for myself in the garden: cutting down a dry pine tree. After tea, as usual these days, read with the daughters on the balcony under the hot rays of sun. The evening was warm and moon-lit.

23rd August. Wednesday.
Today is two years since I arrived in Mogilev. So much water under the bridge since then!
The day stayed magnificent: 23° in the shade, and passed as usual in Tobolsk. Dug up the greenhouse soil in the garden with Kirpichnikov. A warm rain passed.

1st September.
Pankratov, the new Provis. Gov. commissar arrived and settled

in the suite house with his assistant, some unkempt-looking ensign. He has the look of a laborer or an impoverished teacher. He will act as the censor of our mail. The day was cold and rainy.

6th September. Wednesday.
The same kind of a day, and we spent it the same way. Dug up a small duck pond in the garden. The daughters played bumble puppy [tether ball].

7th September. Thursday.
The morning was cloudy and windy, later the weather improved. [We] were outside a lot; filled up the duck pond and sawed up some firewood for our baths.

8th September. Friday.
For the first time went to Blagovesheniye Church, where our priest has been serving for a while now. But my joy was ruined by the foolish incident during our procession over there. Along the path of the town gardens stood the marksmen, and by the church was a huge crowd! This deeply disturbed me. The weather was nice, a little cool.

12th September. Tuesday.
Warm gray day. During the day sawed firewood and the daughters played with tennis balls on the wooden sidewalk.

13th September. Wednesday.
It rained for a half a day but was warm. Finished the book "Na gorakh" [On the Mountains] and started Leskov's novel *Oboydenniye* [The Circumvented]. At 9 o'cl. in the evening there was a *vsenoshnaya* service in our hall. Went to bed early.

14th September. Thursday.
In order to escape the crowds of people in the street by the church, we ordered *obednya* at 8 o'cl. Everything turned out well, the marksmen were arranged along the fence of the town gardens. The weather was bad—cold and damp: but we still got to take a short walk. They allowed Kolya Derevenko to visit Aleksei.

Began in Tobolsk 17th September. Sunday.
Wonderful warm day. 13° in the shade. After *obednitza* took a walk and stayed outside for a long time during the day. Olga stayed in bed with light fever. [General] Tatishev is not completely healthy either.

18th September. Monday. 1917.
The autumn this year is wonderful here: today it was 15° in the shade and completely southern warm air. During the day played *gorodki* [a game] with Valya D.[olgoruky], which I have not done in many, many years. Olga's illness has passed: she sat with Alix on the balcony for a long time. Finished Leskov's "Ostrovityani" [The Islanders]. Wrote a letter to mama under Pankratov's[23] censorship.

24th September. Sunday.
After yesterday's incident they did not allow us to go to church, fearing someone's resentment. *Obednitza* service was at home. The day was superb: 11° in the shade with a warm breeze. Walked for a long time, played *gorodki* with Olga and sawed wood. In the evening read "Zapechatlenniy Angel" aloud.

23. Head of the guards in Tobolsk.

25th September. Monday.
Lovely quiet weather: 14° in the shade. During our walk, the commandant—the dreadful commissar's assistant, ensign Nikolsky and three marksmen from the committee searched all over our house with the purpose of finding wine. Not finding anything, they stayed for a half hour and left. After tea they started to carry in our luggage which arrived from T[sarskoe] S[elo].

26th September. Tuesday.
Another magnificent cloudless day. In the morning walked a lot and read on the balcony before breakfast. Cut wood during the day and played *gorodki*. After tea unpacked the newly arrived rugs and decorated our rooms with them. Finished Leskov's novel *Nekuda* [To Nowhere].

29th September. Friday.
The other day Botkin received a document from Kerensky, from which we found out that we are allowed to take walks outside of town. To Botkin's question as to when this can start, the dreadful Pankratov replied that this is not even up for discussion right now due to some inexplicable concern for our safety. Everyone was extremely indignant by this answer. The weather got cooler. Finished "Ramuntcho."

4th October. Wednesday.
Today we were reminiscing about the convoy holidays in the old times. It was warmer than it sometimes is in Crimea at the same time of year. Good for Tobolsk! Spent the day as usual. After *vsenoshnaya*, Aleksei got his gifts.[24] Had dinner at 7 1/2 o'cl.

24. For his name day.

5th October. Thursday.
Did not get to church for *obednya* on Aleksei's name day due to stubbornness of Mr. Pankratov, and at 11 o'cl. we had a *moleben* service [at the house]. In the morning it was foggy, wh.[ich] dissipated by one o'clock. Spent a long time outside in fresh air. In the evening Aleksei arranged cinematograph for us.

10th October. Tuesday.
The weather remained pleasant—around one degree of frost. Klavdia Mikhailovna Bitner, who arrived here two days ago, gave me the letter from Ksenia. Today she started to tutor the children, except Olga, in various subjects.

20th October. Friday.
Today is the 23rd anniversary of my dear Papa's passing, and in what kind of circumstances we have to live through it! My God, how difficult it is for poor Russia! In the evening before dinner they had a *vsenoshnaya* service for the dead.

21st October. Saturday.
In the morning we saw a funeral procession from the window, with the body of the 4th regiment marksman; in front walking was a small choir of gymnasium students who played badly.

At 11 o'cl. we had the *obednitza* service. Before tea sat at Kostritzky's. At 9 o'cl. had a *vsenoshnaya*, and then we confessed with Father Aleksei. Went to bed early.

2nd November. Thursday.
During the night it abruptly froze up, in the morning [it was] down to 11°. The day was sunny with a northern wind. Took a walk as usual; during the day hauled firewood. In the evening Olga received some modest gifts.

3rd November. Friday.
Dear Olga is 22 years old; pity that the poor thing had to spend her birthday under current circumstances. At 12 o'cl. we had a *moleben*. The weather became mild again. Sawed some wood. Started a new interesting book "The Elusive Pimpernel."

4th November. Saturday.
In the morning I was overjoyed by a letter from Ksenia. There was a lot of snow, shoveled the walking path, and during the day hauled firewood to the shed.

Already for two days the agents' telegrams have not arrived—must be that dire events are happening in big cities! At 9 o'cl. had a *vsenoshnaya*.

14th November. Tuesday.
Birthday of my dear[25] and our 23rd wedding anniversary! At 12 o'cl. *moleben* service; the choristers kept getting confused and making mistakes, must have not practiced. The weather was sunny, warm and with a strong wind. During the afternoon tea I read my old diaries—a pleasant pastime.

17th November. Friday.
The same unpleasant weather with stabbing wind. It is nauseating to read the newspaper descriptions of what happened two weeks ago in Petrograd and Moscow! Much worse and more shameful than the events in the Time of Troubles.

18th November. Saturday.
Received shocking news that 3 members of the parliament of our 5th army went to the Germans ahead of Dvinsk, and signed some preliminary peace treaty with them!

25. Alexandra.

21st November. Tuesday.
We were forced to spend the Temple Entrance Holy Day without a service because Pankratov did not feel like allowing it! The weather was warm. Everyone worked in the yard.

26th November. Sunday.
Today is Georgievsky holiday. The town arranged a dinner for the Cavalry and other entertainments in the People's House. There were a few Georg. cavaliers but in the ranks of our guards whom their non-Cavalry comrades decided not to relieve, and forced them to serve—even on such a day! Liberty!!! Walked a lot and for a long time, the weather was mild.

30th November. Thursday.
A nice clear day −8° of frost. From 12 o'cl before breakfast tutored Aleksei. During the day hauled firewood into the shed. After tea, Olga was playing cards with Aleksei, showed 4 beziques.

1st December. Friday. 2nd December, Saturday.
Both days passed the exact same way. It was rather freezing and sunny. After the afternoon walk we meet at M. Gilliard's [the French tutor] daily, and overtly study our roles.[26] At 9 o'cl. had a *vsenoshnaya*.

6th December. Wednesday.
Spent my name day quietly and not like in the previous years. At 12 o'cl. a *moleben* service. The marksmen of the 4th regiment [were] in the garden, former guards, all congratulated me, and I them—with the regiment holiday.

26. For a play.

Received three name day pies and sent one of them to the guards. In the evening Maria, Aleksei and M. Gilliard acted in a very friendly little play "Le Fluide de John"; there was a lot of laughter.

7th December. Thursday.
The freeze came down to 22° with a strong wind, which cut the face, nevertheless we successfully went outside in the morning and evening. In my study, in the daughters' room and the hall it is very cold −10°, which is why I wear my *Plastun cherkesska*[27] all day until nighttime. Finished part II of "World History."

—

From the memoirs of V. I. Chebotareva:
December.
Strange coincidence: the favorite child[28] of the Toboltzy[29] ceased to exist on the first year anniversary of Grigori's [Rasputin] death. To save everything and store it at the Grand Palace will most likely not be possible; already greedy paws are reaching out from all sides, asking for instruments, beds, linens.

—

From the diary of Nicholas II:
9th December. Saturday.
Got a nice letter from Olga [Alexandrovna]. It got colder, it was windy and clear. After my walk I tutored Aleksei. Finally, after intense heating it got really warm in [our] rooms.

27. Uniform of the unhorsed Cossacks.
28. The palace infirmary where Olga used to work.
29. Refers to the imperial family: "Tobolsk residents."

21st December. Thursday.
The weather was very pleasant. Gave a lesson to Aleksei before breakfast. Wrote to Olga [Alexandrovna] in Ai-Todor.[30] In the evening Anastasia got some modest gifts.

22nd December. Friday.
Celebrated Anastasia's name day with a *moleben* at 12 o'cl. During the day worked on the hill and sawed firewood. After tea we rehearsed.

24th December. Sunday.
In the morning sat at the dentist's for a half hour. At 12 o'cl. there was an *obednitza* service in the hall. Before our walk, prepared gifts for everyone and set up the Christmas trees. During tea—before 5 o'cl.—went with Alix to the guard room and had a party for the 1st platoon of the 4th regiment. Sat with the marksmen of all shifts until 5 1/2 o'cl. After dinner, a party for suite and all our people, and we had ours before 8 o'cl. *Vsenoshnaya* was very late, started at 10 1/2, as the *Batushka* could not make it [earlier] due to the church service. The off-shift marksmen were there.

26th December. Tuesday.
The same kind of quiet frosty day −13°. Everyone slept a lot. In the morning stopped by the guard room with the children—the 1st platoon of the 1st regiment were there; yesterday we sent them a tree, a sweet pie and a checkers game. The other day Isa Buxhoveden arrived, but was not allowed to see us due to Pankratov's caprice.

—

30. In Crimea, where the rest of Nicholas's side of the family was living at the time.

Letter from Olga to her friend Rita Khitrovo:
26 December 1917.
Hello my dear Ritka! Well, the Holidays are upon us already. We have a Christmas tree in the corner of the hall and it dispenses a wonderful scent, but not at all the same as in Tsarskoe [Selo]. This is some special kind of tree called "balsam." It smells strongly of oranges and tangerines, and there is resin flowing down the trunk constantly. There are no ornaments, but only silver streams and wax candles, of course from the church, since there are no other.

—

From the diary of Nicholas II:
28th December. Thursday.
A lovely sunny warm day, 2° of frost. Stayed outside for a long time in the morning and the evening. Resentfully [we] learned that our good Father Aleksei is being investigated and is under house arrest.

This happened because during the *moleben* on 25th Dec, the deacon mentioned us by title while a lot of marksmen of the 2nd regiment were present in the church as usual, and they apparently made a fuss, but [it was] without Pankratov's involvement.

29th December. Friday.
Another nice sunny day, 4° of frost. Worked on the hill which is now ready, and sawed [wood] during the day, while the daughters skied down [the snow hill].

30th December. Saturday.
A clear quiet day. Aleksei's calf is slightly swollen, and he stayed in bed. Walked a lot, the daughters went outside after dinner too.

31st December. Sunday.
Not a cold day [but] with strong wind. Aleksei got up towards the evening since he was able to put on his boots now.

After tea, [we] dispersed before the arrival of the new year.

1918

After the Bolsheviks came to power in October 1917, the conditions of Olga and her family's imprisonment grew stricter, and talk of putting the former tsar on trial got louder. Life for the family became progressively worse in March 1918 when the family was placed on soldiers' rations and hence was forced to part with many of their loyal retainers, who gave them much needed support, because they were unable to feed them. As the civil war between the "Reds" and the "Whites" gained momentum, Lenin's new government increasingly viewed the former tsar and his family as a liability that became a dangerous banner for the monarchists to rally around. In April 1918, Nicholas, Alexandra, and Maria were transferred to Ekaterinburg, a city in the Urals that was extremely hostile to the former tsar. Olga and her two sisters remained in Tobolsk with their ill brother until Aleksei was healthy enough to travel. They joined their parents and sister in Ekaterinburg about a month later.

—

From the diary of Nicholas II:
1st January. Monday.
At 8 o'clocl. went to *obednya* without Olga and Tatiana, unfortunately, because both ended up with fever. The doctors think that most likely it's rubella. A different priest and deacon serviced the *obednya*. The weather was wonderful, really March-like.

2nd January. Tuesday.
Rubella confirmed in both, but happily they feel better today, [but have] a rather glaring rash.

The day was gray. Not cold but with strong wind. Walked in the garden without anything to do—today is green for boredom!

3rd January. Wednesday.
Aleksei also caught rubella, but a very mild one; Olga and Tatiana felt well, the latter even got up. It snowed all day. The marksmen detachment committee ordered me to remove [my] epaulets in order not to be exposed to insults and attacks in town. Incomprehensible!

4th January. Thursday.
Maria got sick today, her face became reddish-purple from the rash, and the fever was high right away. Tatiana got out of bed completely. Walked only with Anastasia. It was 10° of frost and windy. Rehearsed the play. Got a letter from Ksenia.

5th January. Friday.
Almost everyone has recovered; Maria was still in bed for another day. At 3 o'clock we had a *vechernya*[1] service and all the rooms were sprinkled with holy water. Talked with the marksmen of the 1st platoon 4th regiment about the removal of the epaulets and the behavior of the 2nd regiment marksmen, which they strongly disapprove of.

6th January. Epiphany.
At 8 o'clock [when I] went to *obednya*, instead of the *shinel*[2] I wore a [civilian] overcoat. The daughters all recovered but do not all go outside. The weather was holiday-like, sunny, quiet. In the morning sat with the guards for a long time and had a heart-to heart [talk] with them. Unfortunately could

1. Evening prayer service.
2. Military overcoat.

not see the Cross procession to the Irtysh [river] due to the surrounding houses [blocking it].

12th January. Friday.
Celebrated Tatiana's name day with a moleban in the hall at 12 o'clock. The day was wonderful, 14° of frost, with a strong warm sun.

Our priest, Father Aleksei was freed from the house arrest.

———

Letter from Olga to Rita Khitrovo:
We warmly thank you, darling Ritka, for the charming postcards. Hope that you had nice holidays. Ours passed unnoticed, quietly. We now always slide down the [snow] hill which we built in the yard. I already managed to get a bump on my forehead. . . .

[They] play hide-and-seek in the dark, etc. We keep remembering our games at the infirmary and at Anya's house with you.

Was Ksenia[3] accepted into the university? I thank you for the news about N.D.[4] It's time to end, going to supper soon. I kiss you warmly, my darling. May the Lord keep you. 14 January, 1918, from Tobolsk.

———

From the diary of Nicholas II:
15th January. Monday.
Anastasia came down with rubella today. The weather was gray, 4° of frost with some wind. Finished reading Leskov's volume XI.

3. Rita's younger sister.
4. Possibly Olga's one-time crush.

16th January. Tuesday.
Anastasia felt well; temperature 37.4; more rash on her chest
than on her face. The weather was very mild, almost a meltdown. From 4 to 5 o'clock had a lesson with Aleksei. Read
aloud to Anastasia before dinner.

19th January. Friday.
Sunny frosty day; 20°, quiet. Finished all yesterday's written
work in the evening. Anastasia completely recovered and
came downstairs for breakfast. At night [temperature] froze
down to 27°.

29th January. Monday.
Took a walk in the morning. At 11 1/2 had an *obednitza* service at our [house]. Worked in the garden for a long time. The
weather was gray, with 5° of frost, pleasant. After dinner we
had our fourth family play. Olga, Tatiana, Maria and
Nastenka H.[endrikova] and Tatishev acted in "La Bete
Noire" together. It started at 91/4 and ended at 10 o'clock.

18 February (3 March). Sunday.
Had *obednitza* at 11 1/2. The day was wonderful, warm, very
spring-like; meltdown during the day. Sat at Rendel's.
Worked in the garden and sawed. After tea, rehearsal. The
play was on in the evening. At first it was the Engl.[ish]
play—"The Crystal Gazer"—Maria and M. Gibb[e]s, and
then ours—"The Bear," in which Olga, [and] again Maria
and I acted. In the beginning of the show we were nervous,
but I think it all went well.

—

Letter from Olga to Rita Khitrovo:[5]
19th February 1918.
Tobolsk—I apologize for the torn paper, but difficult to write on it.

I was so happy to finally hear from you, my dear Ritka. The letter from 20th Jan. only came today. [I] wrote you some letters on the 11th and 21st Jan. and 3rd Feb. (old style of course), but I don't know if they ever got to you. I feel so sorry for poor Vadya! As far as the fat O., he didn't perish but is ill (had a stroke). His son is there too, [he is] healthy. I just happened to get a letter from them today. It's so horrible what's going on everywhere, but we must hold on to the hope that things will get better. I imagine it was so frightening during those days in Od.[essa?]. God be praised that now it is calm. [illeg.] seems like an eternity since I've had any news from Katya, but this means the letters from there do get to you. Recently Olga Porf. wrote to me, she is happy with her Bar. [?] and I am happy for her. She writes that Krein [?] is alive, he was in Kiev. This was told to her by Kh.[illeg. maybe "surgeon"–"khirurg" ?] who saw him there. Al. Vlad.[imirovich?] is going to Japan, he writes often. You know, Pankr.[atov] is no longer here, only the Colonel is left. Hoping he will stay permanently. The weather is not cold, for two days [it was] overcast and snowing; here everything is [illeg.] a lot, as in Tsarskoe [Selo]. Everything is as always here, so there is absolutely nothing to write about. They do not let us go to church anymore, but all the rest is the same. There is really not much to do, [I] started to chop wood in the garden, but can't say that I am that good at it. Brother [Aleksei] and Kolya Derev.[enko] are digging some sort of ditches and tunnels in the snow, into which you are supposed

5. The last known letter Olga wrote.

to crawl in on your stomach, [they are] very happy with their accomplishments.—[My] hair is growing well, but [all] our hair became very scruffy so we look like ruffians, except for Maria whose hair curls nicely. Of course we don't get it curled.

So what else can I tell you? I think I already wrote about our Sunday plays. They are going well and sometimes it's really funny. That they never did allow Isa to [see] us you already know too. She lives with her old Englishwoman in a private flat, and both of them give someone some sort of lessons and are happy with that. Have not heard from Tilly [?] in a while either and don't know where she is now. Darling, I will write Katya a letter, maybe you will get the chance to somehow forward it to her. At the post office here they do not accept any letters to Petrograd, Moscow and Kiev, but evidently you have not had this mail interruption yet. Did Olga Evgeniyevna leave yet? If not, then tell her that Aunt Olga asked to send her regards. The latter writes [to us] often. She is so blissful with her husband and son. They don't have a nanny, so they do everything themselves for their baby boy. Judging by the pictures he is awfully cute and so big already. Ritka, I won't write to Katya [illeg.], [I] found out about the capture of K. . . . How hard all this is!—To our great disappointment [we] did not receive your packages, except for the first one. And where are Yulia and her husband now [Lillie Dehn?]? [There have been] no letters from Olya for a long time. Today it snowed all day and [is] really warm. Puttered around the hill [snow mountain?] (probably for the last time, evidently they want to put it out to pasture). Ha, ha, ha!!! A lot of stupidity going on in the world! Well, I think this is all the news I have. Vik.[tor?] Yak.[ovlevich?] has not written in a long long time. Please send my regards to your dear landlords [?] and to Little [illeg.] if you see him.

Does he know anything about his [family]? Mine are sending regards and hugs. I kiss you affectionately, my dear, dear Ritka, I love and remember you. Lord keep you. Olga.

—

From the diary of Nicholas II:
2/15 March. Friday.[6]
These days [I am] remembering last year in Pskov and in the train!

How much longer will our poor motherland be tormented and pulled apart by the external and internal enemies? Sometimes it seems that there is no more strength to take this, [I] don't even know what to hope or wish for?

Nevertheless, there is no one like God! May His holy will be served!

8/21 March. Thursday.
Today is a year [anniversary] that I parted from my dear mama in Mogilev and departed for T. Selo. Got a letter from Ksenia. The weather was erratic, first sunny, then snowing, but warm in general.

9/22 March. Friday.
Today is the one year anniversary of my arrival in Tsarskoe Selo and [my] arrest along with the family at the Alexander Palace. Unwittingly one remembers this past difficult year! And what else is awaiting us all in the future? All of it is in God's hands! All our hopes are in Him alone.

At 8 o'clock we went to *obednya*. Spent the day as usual. Had dinner at 7 o'clock, and then had *vechernya* and after that Confessions in the hall—the children's, the suite's, [our] people's and ours.

6. Nicholas is using both the old and new style calendars.

27 March. Tuesday.
The cold came right away with a northern wind. The day remained bright. Yesterday read aloud Niluis' book about the Antichrist to which the "protocols" of the Jews and masons[7] were added—a rather contemporary reading material.[8]

28 March. Wednesday.
An excellent sunny day without any wind. Yesterday we had an alarm among our ranks based on the rumors about additional Red Army soldiers arriving from Ekaterinburg. The guard was doubled at night, the patrol strengthened and the outposts were sent outside. They were talking about alleged danger to us in this house, and of the necessity for transferring [us] to the bishop's house on the hill.

There was talk about this all day among the committee, etc. and finally they all calmed down in the evening, about which Kobilinsky[9] came to report to me at 7 o'clock. They even asked Alix not to sit out on the balcony for three days!

29 March. Thursday.
During the morning walk saw the "special commissar" Demianov, who with his assistant Degtyarev, escorted by the commandant and the marksmen, made the rounds of the guard house and the garden. Because of him, i.e., this Demianov, and the marksmen's unwillingness to miss him, is why all that fuss started three days ago.

30 March. Friday.
A new day, a new surprise! Today Kobilinsky brought a paper

7. *Protocols of the Elders of Zion*, an anti-Semitic forgery, first published in Russia in 1903, purporting to detail a Jewish conspiracy to dominate the world.
8. Yet another example of rampant anti-Semitism among the aristocracy in Russia at the time.
9. The new commandant in Tobolsk.

from Moscow which he received yesterday from the Central Executive Committee [addressed] to our platoon, [an order] to transfer all of our [people] who live in that house to our [house] and consider us under arrest again, as in T. Selo. Right away the transfer of chamber women from one room to another began downstairs, in order to make space for the new arrivals.

Aleksei's groin started to hurt due to coughing, and he was in bed all day.

31 March. Saturday.
He [Aleksei] did not sleep all night and suffered a lot during the day, poor thing. The weather was, as if on purpose, lovely and warm, the snow is melting fast. Walked for a long time. Things and furniture from the Kornilov house was hauled over before breakfast, the residents already made themselves at home in the new building.

1 April. Sunday.
Today it was decided by the rank committee that to be able to execute the order from Moscow that the people residing in our house also were not allowed to go outside, i.e., into town. Therefore all day there was talk of how to fit them all into the already full house, since there were seven people moving in. All this is being done so fast due to the rapidly coming arrival of the new regiment with a commissar who is bringing instructions with him. Therefore our marksmen, to avoid any complaints about them, wish for them to observe strict management!

2 April. Monday.
In the morning, the commandant, with the committee of officers and two marksmen, made partial rounds of our

house. The result of this "search" was the confiscation of the swords from Valya and Mr. Gilliard, and a dagger—from me! Again Kobilinsky explained that this as a necessary measure to calm down the marksmen!

Aleksei felt better, and he fell deeply asleep from 7 o'clock. The weather was gray, quiet.

3 April. Tuesday.
He slept, with some short breaks for twelve hours, almost [had] no pain. The weather was unpleasant, wet snow and cold wind. The day passed as usual.

4 April. Wednesday.
The weather was gray, quiet, the sun came out at around 4 o'clock. Walked for an hour in the morning, and walked and sawed wood during the day for two hours. Aleksei is better, but he is tired of lying down in the same position; [had] fever, as yesterday, is not high—38.4. [*sic*] Vl.[adimir] Nikol.[aevich] Derevenko feels that this kind of temp. is necessary, since it assists in getting the swelling down.

8 April. Sunday.
Twenty fourth anniversary of our engagement! The day was sunny, with a cold wind, all the snow melted.

At 11 1/2 there was *obednitza*. After Kobilinsky showed me the telegram from Moscow, which confirmed the decision of the rank committee about the removal of my and Aleksei's epaulets!

Therefore I decided not to wear them for my walks but only wear them at home. I will never forgive them this swinishness! Worked in the garden for two hours. In the evening read aloud "Volkhvy"—also by Vsevolod Soloviev.

—

From the memoirs of Anna Vyrubova:

I believed that soon there will be a reaction and the Russian people will realize their mistake and sins towards our dear captives in Tobolsk.

Of the same mind was even the revolutionary Burtzev, whom I met at a relative's house, and the writer [Maxim] Gorky who, most likely out of curiosity, wanted to see me.

Hoping to save Their Majesties, or at least improve their conditions, I threw myself at anyone. I myself went to see him so that my own location did not become known. For more than two hours I spoke with this strange man, who on the one hand seemed to stand behind the Bolsheviks, but at the same time expressed disgust and openly criticized their politics, terror and tyranny.

He expressed his deep disappointment in the revolution and in the way that the Russian workers behaved themselves after getting their long awaited liberty.

What he said about the Tsar and the Tsarina filled my heart with joyful hope. According to his words they were the victims of the revolution and fanaticism of the current times, and after thoroughly looking over the imperial quarters at the palace they seemed [to him] not even aristocrats but a simple bourgeois family, with an impeccable lifestyle.

He told me that on me lay the responsibility—to write the truth about Their Majesties "to make peace between the Tsar and his people." . . .

I saw him twice more and showed him a few pages from my memoirs, but it was impossible to write in Russia.

The fact that I met with Gorky was screamed about by those who did not grow tired of ruining my reputation, but later all the unfortunates went to him for assistance [too]. . . .

——

From the diary of Nicholas II:
9 April. Monday.
Found out about the arrival of the special authorized [person] Yakovlev from Moscow; he moved into the Kornilov house. The children imagined that he will show up today to do a search and burned all letters, and Maria and Anastasia also [burned] their diaries. The weather was disgusting, cold and with wet snow. Aleksei felt better and even slept during the day for about two–three hours.

10 April. Tuesday.
At 10 1/2 o'clock in the morning Kobilinsky showed up with Yakovlev and his entourage. I received him in the hall with the daughters. We expected him at 11 o'clock, which was why Alix was not yet ready.

He came in, clean shaven, smiling and embarrassed, asked if I was happy with the guards and the premises. Then, almost running, he went in to see Aleksei, without stopping looked over the rest of the rooms and, apologizing for troubling us, went downstairs. In a similar rush he stopped by all the rest [of the rooms] on other floors.

In a half hour he showed up again in order to introduce himself to Alix, again hurried to Aleksei's [room] and went downstairs. This was the extent of [his] review of the house for now.

[I] took a walk as usual; the weather was irregular, first sun then snow.

12 April. Thursday.
After breakfast Yakovlev came over with Kobilinsky and announced that he got an order to take me away, without telling us where?

Alix decided to go with me and take Maria; there was no point in protesting. It was more than difficult to leave the rest of the children and Aleksei—sick and under current circumstances!

We started to pack all the most necessary things immediately. Then Yakovlev said that he will return for O., T., An. and A., and that most likely we will see them in about three weeks. Spent a sad evening; of course no one slept that night.

13 April. Friday.
At 4 o'clock said goodbye to our dear children and climbed into the *tarantasses:*[10] I—with Yakovlev, Alix—with Maria, Valya—with Botkin.

From our people, the following went with us: Nyuta [Anna] Demidova, Chermodurov and Sednev,[11] 9 marksmen and cavalry convoy (Red Army) of 10 men.

The weather was cold with an unpleasant wind, the road was very bad, and awfully bumpy from the frozen tracks. Crossed Irtysh in rather deep water. Changed horses four times, making 130 *versts* the first day.

Came to Ievlevo village to spend the night. Got settled in a large clean house; slept deeply on our cots.

14 April. Saturday.
Got up at 4 o'clock since we had to depart at 5 o'clock, but there was a delay, because Yakovlev slept late, and besides he was waiting for a lost package.

Walked across Tobol on planks, but on the other bank had to ride about 10 *sazhens*[12] on a ferry. Met Yakovlev's assistant—Guzakov, who was in charge of the guards on the way to Tyumen.

10. Type of flat sleigh.
11. All three servants mentioned here were murdered along with the imperial family in July 1918.
12. About seventy feet; one sazhen equals seven feet.

The day was beautiful and very warm, the road became more smooth; but it was still very bumpy, and I was concerned for Alix. It was very dusty in the open spaces, and dirty in the woods.

Changed horses in Pokrovskoye village, we stood for a long time right across from Grigori's house and saw his whole family who looked out the windows.[13]

The last change of horses was in Borky village. Here, E. S. Botkin developed very bad kidney pains, he was put to bed in the house for an hour and a half, and then he moved forward slowly.

We had tea and snacks with our people and the marksmen in the village's school building. The last stage [of the trip] was slow and with all sorts of military precautionary measures.

Arrived in Tyumen at 91/4 in the beautiful moonlight with the entire squadron which surrounded our carts at the entrance into town. It was pleasant to end up on the train, even though it was not very clean; we ourselves and our things had made an awfully dirty sight.

Went to bed at 10 o'clock without undressing, I—above Alix's bunk, Maria and Nyuta in the adjoining compartment.

15 April. Sunday.
Everyone slept well. Figured out by the name of the stations that we are heading towards Omsk. Started to guess: where will they take us after Omsk? Toward Moscow or toward Vladivostok? The commissars said nothing of course.

Maria went to see the marksmen often—their compartment was at the end of the train car, there were four [men] there, the rest were in the adjacent car.

Had dinner at the stop, the station Vagai at 11 o'clock, very delicious. Closed curtains at the stations, because due to

13. Rasputin's hometown.

a holiday there were a lot of people. After a cold snack with tea went to bed early.

16 April. Monday.
In the morning noticed that we were heading back. Turned out that they did not want to let us through in Omsk! At least it became freer for us, even took a walk twice, the first time along the train, and the second—rather far away in a field with Yakovlev himself. Everyone was in a good mood.

17 April. Tuesday.
Such a wonderful warm day. At 8.40 arrived in Ekaterinburg. Stood at one station for about three hours. There was some serious quarrelling between the locals and our commissars. In the end the former won out, and the train went to another— commercial train station.

After an hour and a half of standing, we came out of the train. Yakovlev transferred us to the local regional commissar with whom the three of us climbed into a motor [car] and rode through deserted streets to the house prepared for us— Ipatiev's. One by one our people and also the luggage arrived, but they did not allow Valya through.

The house is nice, clean. We were allotted four large rooms: a corner bedroom, bathroom, dining room nearby with windows looking out on a garden and the view of the lower part of town, and finally, a spacious hall with an arch without a door.

We could not unpack for a long time as the commissar and the officer of the guard were not able to start the search of the chests.[14] And the search was similar to customs, very thorough, right down to the last jar in Alix's travel first aid kit.

14. Their luggage.

This [made me] explode [in] anger, and I bluntly gave the commissar a piece of my mind. At 9 o'clock we finally settled in. Had dinner from the hotel at 4 1/2 and after a clean-up had a snack with tea.

Settled in this way: Alix, Maria and I, all three in the bedroom, the bathroom is common, N. Demidova—in the dining room, Botkin, Chermodurov, and Sednev—in the hall.

In order to go to the bathroom and the W.C. we had to pass by the sentry at the door of the guard room. Around the house they built a very high plank fence two *sazhen* away from the windows; a chain of sentries stood there, and in the garden also.

18th April. Wednesday.
Slept wonderfully. Had tea at 9 o'clock. Alix stayed in bed in order to rest from all she went through.

In honor of 1 May listened to the music of some parade. We were not allowed to go out to the garden today!

I wanted to take a good bath, but the plumbing was not working, and they could not bring water in a barrel. This is so tiresome as my feeling of cleanliness definitely suffered.

The weather was wonderful, bright and sunny, it was 15° in the shade, [we] breathed in fresh air through an open window vent.

19 April. Holy Thursday.
The day was excellent, windy, the dust was flying around the whole town, the sun burned through the windows.

In the morning I read a book to Alix, "La Sagesse et la Destinee" [by] Maeterlinck. Later continued the reading of the Bible. Breakfast was brought late—at 2 o'clock. Then we all, except Alix, took advantage of permission to go outside into the garden for an hour.

The weather got cooler, there were even a few rain drops. It was nice to breathe some fresh air. It was sad hearing the [church] bells, thinking that this is the Passion [week] and we do not have the opportunity to go to these wonderful services, and besides we cannot even fast. Before tea I had the pleasure of taking a substantial bath.

20th April. Holy Friday.
It got a lot colder overnight: instead of rain it was snowing occasionally, but it immediately melted. The sun came out sporadically.

Our guard did not change for two days for some reason. Now their premises are located on the lower floor, which is undoubtedly more comfortable for us—we don't have to walk past all of them to the W.C. or washroom and it no longer smells of smoke in the dining room.

Dinner was very late due to the pre-holiday rush of food supplies in town; sat down to dinner at 3 1/2 o'cl. Then walked with Maria and Botkin for a half hour. Had tea at 6 o'cl.

In the mornings and evenings, as usual these days here, read appropriate passages from the Holy Bible aloud in the bedroom.

By the ambiguous hints of those around us we understood that poor Valya is not free and that he will be investigated, after which he will be set free![15] There was no opportunity to get into any kind of contact with him, no matter how hard Botkin tried.

21 April. Holy Saturday.
Woke up rather late; the day was gray, cold, with snow-storms. Read aloud all morning, added a few lines to the

15. Valya Dolgoruky was executed by the Bolsheviks in 1918.

daughters in Alix's and Maria's letters and drew the plan of this house.[16]

Had dinner at one 1/2. Took a walk for 20 minutes. By Botkin's request they allowed a priest and a deacon to come to us at 8 o'cl. They did a morning service fast and well; it was a huge consolation to pray in this environment and hear "Christ has risen." Ukraintsev, the commandant's assistant, and the guards were present. After the service we had supper and went to bed early.

22 April. Holy Christ has Risen.
Heard the popping of fireworks all evening and part of the night, which they fired off in different parts of town.

During the day it was freezing, around 3°, and the weather was gray. In the morning we exchanged triple kisses amongst ourselves and ate *kulich*[17] and red eggs with tea,— could not get a *paskha*.[18]

Had dinner and supper at the usual time. Walked for a half hour. In the evening chatted with Ukraintsev for a long time in Botkin's [room].

30 April. Monday.
The day was excellent, clear. Took a walk in the morning for an hour. Dinner was unconscionably late, they brought it at 3 1/2! Therefore we went for our second walk only at about 4 o'cl.

Some old woman, and then a boy, got close to the fence— to stare at us through a hole; they tried to shoo them away but everyone laughed while doing it.

The idiot Avdeyev came to the garden but kept his distance. Had supper at 8 1/2 o'cl. Read aloud a lot during the

16. On this page of the diary there was a hand-drawn plan of the house marked "The Ipatiev House in Ekaterinburg" in Nicholas II's hand.
17. Easter bread.
18. Special Easter cake.

day, nice stories by Leykin, "The Optimistic Russians." In the evening—bezique with Alix.

1 May. Tuesday.
We were overjoyed by the letters received from Tobolsk; I got one from Tatiana [Konstantinovna]. We read each other's letters all morning. The weather was great, warm.

The guard was changed at noon, from the ranks of the same special frontier team—Russians and Latvians. The head—[is] a presentable young man.

Today they told us through Botkin that we are only allowed to walk one hour per day; and to the question why? the acting commandant replied "So that it is similar to a prison schedule."

Food came on time. They bought us a samovar—at least we won't be dependent on the guards now [for tea]. In the evening had four beziques [wins] during the game.

2 May. Wednesday.
The application of the "prison mode" continued and expressed itself in that an old painter had painted over all our windows in all the rooms with lime. It started to feel like fog behind the windows.

Went to walk at 3 1/2 and at 4.10 they chased us inside. There was not one extra soldier in the garden. The head guard did not speak to us since all this time one of the commissars was in the garden watching us, him and the guard!

The weather was very nice, but the rooms got gloomy. Only the dining room won out because they took down the rug outside the window!

Sednev[19] has a cold with fever.

---

19. The imperial family's cook who voluntarily went into exile with them and was also executed.

3 May. Thursday.
The day was gray but warm. One could feel the dampness in the rooms especially our two [rooms]; the air entering the window vent was warmer than inside. I taught Maria to play trick-track.

Sednev's fever is better, but he stayed in bed all day. Walked for exactly an hour. The guard order significantly increased, there were no more loiterers in the garden with us.

During the day we got coffee, Easter eggs and chocolate from Ella in Perm. We lost electricity in the dining room, had supper with two candles in jars. In the hall not everything had electricity either. Took a bath after Maria at 7 1/2 o'cl.

4 May. Friday.
It rained all day. Found out that the children left Tobolsk, but Avdeyev didn't tell us when. He also opened the door to the locked room which was intended by us for Aleksei. It turned out to be large and brighter than we expected since it has two windows; our stove heats it well.

Walked for a half hour due to rain. There was plenty of food as usual, and [it] came in time. The commandant, his assistant, the head guard and the electricians ran around all the rooms, fixing wires, despite which we [still] supped in the dark.

6 May. Sunday.
I have lived to 50 years old, it even feels strange to myself!

The weather was great, as if on order. At 11 1/2 the same priest with the deacon did a *moleben* service, which was very nice.

Took a walk with Maria before dinner. During the day sat in the garden for an hour and a quarter, warming in the sun.

We are not getting any news from the children and started to doubt, did they really leave Tobolsk?

8 May. Tuesday.
Heard thunder in the morning; [a storm] passed outside the city, but we had a few downpours. Read before dinner, the 4th part of *War and Peace*, which [I] never knew before.

Walked for an hour with Maria. Avdeyev offered us to look at two rooms next to the dining room; the guards are now located in the cellar. Waited for dinner and supper for more than half hour. Received a congratulatory telegram from Olga for 6th May [his birthday].

10 May. Thursday.
In the morning they intermittently announced to us that the children are a few hours from the city, then that they have arrived at the station, and finally that they have arrived at the house, although their train was already standing here since 2 o'cl. in the morning! What enormous joy it was to see them again and to hug them after four weeks of being apart and the uncertainty.

There was no end to the mutual questions and answers. Very few letters got to them and from them. They went through a lot of emotional suffering in Tobolsk, the poor things, and during the three-day trip.

It snowed overnight and [snow] was on the ground all day. From everyone who arrived with them they only allowed in the cook Kharitonov and Sednev's nephew.

During the day we went out to the garden for about 20 minutes—it was cold and terribly dirty. Waited for the arrival of the beds from the train station until nighttime, but in vain, and all the daughters were forced to sleep on the floor.

Aleksei spent the night on Maria's bed. In the evening, to make things even worse, he bruised his knee and suffered all night and did not let us sleep.

11 May. Friday.
Waited for our people from Tobolsk to be allowed in since morning and the arrival of the rest of the baggage. Decided to let my old man Chermodurov off for a rest and instead of him take in Trupp temporarily.

They let him and Nagorny come in only in the evening, and for an hour and a half they questioned and searched them in the commandant's room.

Although we were all sitting together in the bedroom, I read a lot; started Apukhtin's *The Unfinished Novel*.

12 May. Saturday.
Everyone slept well, except Aleksei, who was moved to his own room yesterday. He continues to have terrible pains, which are alleviated periodically.

The weather was completely appropriate for our mood, wet snow with 3° of warmth. We conducted talks though Evg.[eni] S.[ergeyevich][20] with the head of the Regional Soviet about allowing M. Gilliard to us.

The children unpacked some of their things after an unbelievably long search of them in the commandant's room. Walked for about 20 minutes.

13 May. Sunday.
Slept wonderfully, except Aleksei. His pains persist, but with long breaks. He stayed in bed in our room. There was no [religious] service.

The weather was the same, snow on the roofs. As in all the recent days, V. N. Derevenko came to examine Aleksei; today a dark gentleman was accompanying him, in whom we recognized a doctor.[21]

20. Dr. Evgeni Botkin.
21. In fact, this was Yakov Yurovsky (1878–1938), a Bolshevik commissar in charge of the "House of Special Purpose" in Ekaterinburg. He was the chief executioner of Nicholas II and his family.

After a short walk we entered a barn with commandant Avdeyev, where our large baggage was dropped off. The search of some unopened chests continued.

Started to read the works of Saltykov [Shedrin] from the bookcase of the owner of the house. In the evening played bezique.

15 May. Tuesday.
Today is a month since our arrival here. Aleksei feels the same—only the rest breaks were longer. The weather was hot, stuffy, but cool inside. Had dinner at 2 o'clock. Walked and sat in the garden an hour and 1/4. Alix cut my hair successfully.

25 May. Friday.
Spent dear Alix's birthday in bed with bad pains in my legs and other places.[22] The next two days were better, was able to eat sitting up in a chair.

27 May. Sunday.
Finally got up and left the bed. The day was summery. Took turns walking: Alix, Aleksei, Olga and Maria before dinner; I, Tatiana and Anastasia before tea.

The greenery is nice and succulent, smells nice. Reading Saltykov's 12th volume with interest: "Pshekhonskaya Starina." [The Elders from Psekohn]

28 May. Monday.
A very warm day. They are constantly opening boxes in the barn where our things are located and taking out various objects and provisions from Tobolsk. And that, with no explanation of the reasons. All this makes one think that

22. Nicholas suffered from severe hemorrhoids.

things that are liked can easily be taken to [someone's] homes, which means gone for us! Disgusting!

The external relations have also changed in the past few weeks: the jailers are trying not to talk to us, as if they feel guilty, and it feels like they have some anxiety or are afraid of something. Confusing!

29 May. Tuesday.
Dear Tatiana turned 21! From last night a strong wind was blowing right into the window vent, thanks to which the air in our bedroom finally became clean and rather cool. Read a lot. Again took turns walking.

5 June. Tuesday.
Dear Anastasia turned 17 already. The heat outside and inside was great. Continue reading 3rd volume of Saltykov— engaging and intelligent.

The entire family walked before tea. Since yesterday Kharitonov has been cooking our food, they bring provisions every two days.

The daughters are learning to cook from him and are kneading dough in the evenings, and bake the bread in the morning! Not bad!

14 June. Thursday.
Our dear Maria turned 19. The weather was still tropical, 26° in the shade, and 24° inside the rooms, so difficult to tolerate! Spent a disturbing night and stayed up, dressed. . . .

This all happened because the other day we received two letters, one after the other, where they notified us to be ready to be kidnapped by some loyal people! But the days passed and nothing happened, while the waiting and the uncertainty were very grueling.

21 June. Thursday.[23]

There was a change of commandants today—during dinner Beloborodov and others came in and announced that instead of Avdeyev, the one whom we mistook for a doctor has been appointed—Yurovsky.

During the day before tea, he and his assistants catalogued the gold jewelry—ours and the children's; the majority (rings, bracelets, etc.) they took with them. They explained that it was because there was an unpleasant incident in our house, mentioned our missing things. So the conviction about which I wrote on 28 May had been confirmed.

I feel sorry for Avdeyev, it is not his fault that he was not able to hold back his people from stealing from the chests in the barn.

23. This was Nicholas II's last diary entry.

EPILOGUE

The sweltering night of July 16–17, 1918, marked the end for Olga and her family and for the Romanov dynasty. That night all the members of Olga's immediate family, as well as their "people"—those who voluntarily chose to share their fate in exile—perished in a hail of bullets in a small cellar room of the Ipatiev house in Ekaterinburg. Known as "The House of Special Purpose," it was the last residence of the last Russian tsar and his family. It was also their place of execution. No one was spared.

The family all died at almost the same moment. Their bodies were then scorched with sulfuric acid, broken down with bayonets, and dumped in a common shallow grave just outside of Ekaterinburg. The location of the burial site remained unknown for sixty-one years, until their skeletal remains were found by a dedicated team of people who wanted to get answers and give them to the world.

Much has been written and said about that cruel July night through the years. Those few hours in Russian history became some of the most controversial. Prior to the discovery and identification of the imperial remains, many attempts were made to accurately re-create the events in the cellar of the House of Special Purpose; and most important, to figure out what exactly happened to the bodies of the last Russian imperial family.

After the first set of remains was identified using DNA testing, the scientific community and the majority of the world were convinced that the Grand Duchess Olga, her parents, and two of her three sisters were finally found. However, until just a few years ago, a nagging question remained as to what actually happened to the two missing bodies, Olga's fourteen-year-old brother, Aleksei, and one of her two younger sisters, either Maria or Anastasia.

That last piece of the puzzle was solved in 2007 when the remains of a teenage boy and girl were finally discovered in the Urals, not far from the shallow grave where the original skeletal remains were found. The former were positively identified as Aleksei and one of the younger sisters.

The remains of Nicholas, Alexandra, and their three daughters were interred at the Peter and Paul Cathedral in St. Petersburg alongside of their royal ancestors. At the time of this book's writing the remains of the other two children have not been reburied, but the entire Romanov family is now accounted for. A bleak chapter of Russian history can be closed.

THE RUSSIAN IMPERIAL FAMILY
AND THEIR CIRCLE

Aleksei Nikolaevich, Tsarevich (1904–1918). Heir to the Russian throne. Olga's brother.

Alexander II, Emperor. "Great-grandpa" (1818–1881). Nicholas II's grandfather. Assassinated by a terrorist.

Alexander III, Emperor. "Grandpa" (1845–1894). Nicholas's father.

Alexander Mikhailovich, Grand Duke. "Uncle Sandro" (1866–1933). Husband of Grand Duchess Ksenia Aleksandrovna.

Alexandra Fedorovna, Empress of Nicholas II (1872–1918). Former Princess Alix of Hesse. Olga's mother.

Anastasia Nikolaevna, Grand Duchess. "Shvybz," "Nastasia." (1901–1918). Olga's youngest sister.

Andrei Vladimirovich, Grand Duke (1879–1956). Son of Grand Duke Vladimir Alexandrovich. Nicholas's first cousin.

Battenberg, Victoria, Princess of Battenburg. "Aunt Victoria." Empress Alexandra's sister.

Boris Vladimirovich, Grand Duke.

Botkin, Evgeni Sergeyevich (1865–1918). Court physician. Went into exile with the imperial family and was murdered along with them.

Buxhoeveden, Sophia, Baroness. "Isa" (1884–1956). Lady-in-waiting to Alexandra.

Chebotareva, Valentina Ivanovna. Fellow nurse and friend to the grand duchesses.

Dehn, Lili. Lady-in-waiting to Empress Alexandra.

Demenkov, Nikolai Dmitrievich. Favorite officer and love interest of Grand Duchess Maria Nikolaevna.

Derevenko, Nikolai Vladimirovich. "Kolya." Aleksei's playmate.

Derevenko, Vladimir Nikolaevich. Court physician, Kolya's father.

Dmitri Pavlovich, Grand Duke (1891–1941). Son of Grand Duke Pavel Alexandrovich, first cousin to Nicholas II. Involved in Rasputin's murder.

Dolgorukov, Vasiliy Alexandrovich, Prince. "Valya" (1868–1918) Followed the imperial family into exile, was murdered by the revolutionaries.

"Elena." KR's daughter-in-law.

Elizaveta Feodorovna, Grand Duchess. "Aunt Ella" (1864–1918). Former Princess Ella of Hesse, Empress Alexandra's sister. Was married to the late Grand Duke Sergei Alexandrovich, Nicholas's uncle.

Elizaveta Mavrikievna, Grand Duchess. "Aunt Mavra," née Princess of Saxen-Altenburg. KR's wife.

Fredericks, Vladimir Borisovich (1838–1927). Minister of the Imperial Court.

Gedroitz, V. I. Princess. Medical doctor at the infirmary where Olga worked.

George Mikhailovich, Grand Duke (1862–1919). First cousin to Nicholas II's father, Alexander III.

Georgiy Konstantinovich, Grand Duke. "Uncle Georgiy." Son of Grand Duke Konstantin (KR).

Gibbes, Sidney. English tutor to the imperial children.

Gilliard, Pierre. "Zhilik." French tutor to the imperial children.

Hendrikova, Anastasia Vasilyevna. "Nastia," "Nastenka" (1887–1918). Lady-in-waiting to Empress Alexandra and friend of the imperial family who followed them into exile and was murdered by the revolutionaries.

Henrikova, Countess. Nastenka's mother.

Ioann Konstantinovich, Prince. "Ioannchik" (1886–1918). Son of Konstantin Konstantinovich (KR).

Irina Alexandrovna, Grand Duchess (1895–1970). Daughter of Grand Duchess Ksenia, niece of Nicholas II and Olga's first cousin. Married to Felix Yusupov.

Kharitonov, Ivan Mikhailovich. Cook to the imperial family in exile. Was murdered along with them in July 1918.

Khitrovo, Margarita. "Ritka" (1895–1952). Lady-in-waiting and friend of Olga Nikolaevna.

Kiknadze, Vladimir. "K" of the 3rd Regiment of his Imperial Majesty. A Georgian and favorite of Grand Duchess Tatiana.

Konstantin Konstantinovich. "Uncle Kostya" Nicholas's second cousin (known as KR).

Ksenia Alexandrovna, Grand Duchess (1875–1960). Nicholas's sister.

Kyril Vladimirovich, Grand Duke. "Uncle Kyril" (1876–1938). Nicholas's cousin.

Maria Alexandrovna, Empress. "Great–grandma" (1824–1880). First wife of Alexander II, Nicholas's grandmother.

Maria Feodorovna, Dowager Empress. "Grandma" (1847–1928). Nicholas's mother.

Maria Nikolaevna, Grand Duchess. "Mashka" (1899–1918). Olga's middle sister.

Maria Pavlovna the Elder, Grand Duchess. "Aunt Miechen" (1854–1920). Grand Duke Vladimir Alexandrovich's wife.

Maria Pavlovna, Grand Duchess. "Maria Pavlovna the Younger" (1890–1958). Daughter of Grand Duke Pavel Alexandrovich. Sister of Grand Duke Dmitri Pavlovich. Nicholas's first cousin.

Michael Alexandrovich, Grand Duke. "Uncle Misha" (1878–1918). Youngest brother of Nicholas II.

Nagorny, Klementy G. Sailor nanny to Tsarevich Aleksei.

Nicholas II, Alexandrovich. "Papa" (1868–1918). Last tsar and last Romanov ruler.

Nikolai Nikolaevich, Grand Duke. Former commander in chief of the Russian army.

Olga Alexandrovna, Grand Duchess. "Aunt Olga" (1882–1960). Younger sister of Nicholas II.

Olga Nikolaevna, Grand Duchess (1895–1918).

Orbeliani, Sonia, Princess. Georgian friend of the imperial family.

Paley, Olga, Countess. Morganatic wife of Grand Duke Pavel Alexandrovich. Mother of Prince Vladimir Pavlovich Paley.

Paley, Vladimir Pavlovich, Prince (1897–1918). Son of Grand Duke Pavel Alexandrovich and his morganatic wife Olga Paley. First cousin to Nicholas II.

Pavel Alexandrovich, Grand Duke (1860–1919). Nicholas's uncle, brother of Tsar Alexander III, Dmitri Pavlovich's and Marie Pavlovna (the Younger)'s father.

Rasputin, Dmitri. "Mitya." Son of Grigori Rasputin.

Rasputin, Grigori Yefimovich (1872–1916). Spiritual advisor to the imperial couple. Murdered by Felix Yusupov, et al.

Rasputina, Maria. "Matriona." Daughter of Grigori Rasputin.

Rasputina, Paraskovia. Wife of Grigori Rasputin.

Rasputina, Varvara. "Varya." Daughter of Grigori Rasputin.

Sablin, Nikolai Pavlovich. Admiral. Nicholas's aide-de-camp.

Schneider, Catherine Adolfovna, "Trina." Lady-in-waiting to Empress Alexandra.

Shakh-Bagov, Dmitri. "Mitya." Ensign of His Majesty's Guard's Yerivan 13th Guards Grenadier Regiment. Love interest of Grand Duchess Olga Nikolaevna.

Stolypina, O. B. Widow of Prime Minister Pyotr Arkadievich Stolypin, who was assassinated at a theater in Kiev in 1911 in front of the tsar and his two eldest daughters.

Stürmer, Boris (1848–1917). Prime minister, foreign minister, and interior minister for several months during 1916.

Tatiana Konstantinovna. KR's daughter, Olga's second cousin.

Tatiana Nikolaevna, Grand Duchess (1899–1918). Nearest sister to Olga in age, part of "we 2."

Tatishev, Ilya Leonidovitch, Count.

Victoria Melita, Grand Duchess. "Aunt Ducky." Kyril Vladimirovich's wife, first cousin of Empress Alexandra.

Voronov, Pavel. "Darling Sh." Officer, one of Olga's love interests.

Vyrubova, Anna, née Taneyeva. "Anya" (1884–1964). Close friend of Empress Alexandra.

Yaklovev Vasiliy. Commissar "extraordinaire," transferred Nicholas, Alexandra, and Maria from Tobolsk to Ekaterinburg.

Yurovsky, Yakov (1878–1938). Bolshevik commissar in charge at Ekaterinburg. One of the chief executioners of the former imperial family.

Yusupov, Felix Felixovich. Prince. Husband of Olga's first cousin Irina Alexandrovna. One of Rasputin's murderers.

Yusupova, Irina Alexandrovna. Daughter of Nicholas II's sister Grand Duchess Ksenia. Olga's first cousin.

GLOSSARY OF RUSSIAN TERMS

batushka	Father/priest
bloshki	tiddly winks game
Khristovaniye	Orthodox Easter service
kolorito	a game
kulich	Easter bread
Moleben	supplicatory prayer service used within the Orthodox Church in honor of Jesus Christ, the Mother of God, a feast, or a particular saint or martyr
Nizhnegorodetz	from Nizhny Novgorod
obednya	midday prayer service
Panikhida	Orthodox prayer for the dead
paskha	special Easter cake
sazhen	unit of measurement, about seven feet
staritza	female elder or holy woman
strannitza	female religious pilgrim
vechernya	evening prayer service
versta	obsolete unit of length (equal to 3,500 feet or just over 1 kilometer)
vsenoshnaya	vespers
Yerevantzy	from Yerevan
Znamenie	name of the church in Tsarskoe Selo

BIBLIOGRAPHY

Buchanan, M. *Recollections of Imperial Russia*. Charleston, SC: Nabu Press. 2011.

Chebotareva, V. "Memoirs of the Palace Infirmary" (online source) http://www.proza.ru/2011/11/29/900.

Eagar, M. *Six Years at the Russian Court*. Bowmanville, Ontario: Gilbert's Books, 2011.

Heresh, E. *Tsesarevich Aleksei*. Moscow: Phoenix, 1998.

Kerensky, A. F. *Tragediya Dinastii Romanovykh* (The Tragedy of Romanov Dynasty). Moscow: Tsentrpoligraf, 2005.

Kravtsova, Marina. "Olga Romanova: The Grand Duchess with a Crystal Soul." http://www.pravda.ru/faith/faithculture/02-07-2012/1120875-olga_romanova-0/.

Potts, D. M. *Queen Victoria's Gene: Haemophilia and the Royal Family*. Gloucestershire, UK: Sutton Publishing, 1995.

Romanov, Nicholas. *Dnevniki i dokumenty iz lichnogo arkhiva Nikolaya II* (Diaries and Archives from the Personal Archive of Nicholas II). Moscow: Harvest, 2003.

———. *Dnevniki Imperatora Nikolaya II* (The Diaries of Emperor Nicholas II). Edited by K. F. Shatsillo. Moscow: Orbita, 1991.

Ryabov, G. *Kak Eto Bylo. Romanovy: Sokrytie Tel, Poisk, Posledstviya* (How It Happened. The Romanovs: Exhumation of the Remains, the Search, the Consequences). Moscow: Politburo, 1998.

Spiridovitch, A. *Les Dernières Années de la Cour de Tzarskoe Selo* (Last Years of the Court at Tsarskoe Selo). Paris: Payot, 1929.

Vyrubova, A. *Freilina Yeyo Velichestva: "Dnevnik" i Vospominaniya Anny Vyrubovoy* (Her Majesty's Lady in Waiting: "The Diary" and Memoirs of Anna Vyrubova). Moscow: Sovetsky Pisatel, 1990.

Zvereva, N. K. *Avgusteishie Sestry Miloserdia* (The August Sisters of Mercy). Moscow: Veche Pubishing, 2006.

ACKNOWLEDGMENTS

The author would like to thank the following people:
Anne Lloyd and Ed Voves for their input and encouragement, every step of the way; Lee Weinstein for proofreading and helpful suggestions; Rob Moshein for his useful advice; Jeanne King and Daniel Nadel for their assistance with the manuscript.

Thanks, too, to Svetlana Belkina and especially Antonina Voronskaya, for their help with Olga's coded diary writing. Larisa Rogovaya, Assistant Director at GARF, and other GARF staff members, for their time and kind cooperation. I would also like to acknowledge E. C. S. Banks for kindly allowing me to translate and include Olga's last letter.

To my friends and fellow Russian history buffs: Cheryl Adams Rychkova, Margarita Nelipa, Jan Henkes, Laura Mabee, Lori Stuart, Eva McDonald, Simon Donoghue, Gerjo Slendebroek, and Janet Rasmussen—thank you all for your support and reassurance.

Special thanks to Galina Fomina for her early invaluable assistance with deciphering Olga's handwriting and translations. Also thanks to Anne Lloyd and Kori Roff Lawrence for their generous assistance with the photographs, and to Bob Atchinson for all the valuable resources on his Web site, The Alexander Palace Time Machine (http://www.alexander-palace.org/palace/).

Many thanks to Noreen Abel-O'Connor for her copy editing, Trudi Gershenov for her cover design, and Bruce H. Franklin of Westholme Publishing.

And finally, thanks to all the fans of the "Olga's Diaries" Facebook page for your continued interest.

I would like to dedicate this book to my paternal grandparents, who were both born in Russia in 1918.

INDEX